Where Was Jesus Crucified?

Where Was Jesus Crucified?

Texts, Archaeology, and a New Case for Golgotha on Jerusalem's West Side

TODD M. WEST

With a Foreword by James D. Tabor

RESOURCE *Publications* · Eugene, Oregon

WHERE WAS JESUS CRUCIFIED?
Texts, Archaeology, and a New Case for Golgotha on Jerusalem's West Side

Resource Publications
An Imprint of Wipf and Stock Publishers
199 W. 8th Ave., Suite 3
Eugene, OR 97401

www.wipfandstock.com

PAPERBACK ISBN: 979-8-3852-7138-2
HARDCOVER ISBN: 979-8-3852-7139-9
EBOOK ISBN: 979-8-3852-7140-5

Contents

Foreword

FOR THE PAST 150 years, the quest to identify the historical location of Golgotha has been defined by a deep tension between centuries of ecclesiastical tradition and the unfolding discoveries of modern archaeology. The vast majority of Christians today revere the Church of the Holy Sepulcher as the place of Jesus' crucifixion, a site identified in 326 CE by Queen Helena, mother of the emperor Constantine, and Bishop Macarius of Jerusalem. Others, seeking a more evocative experience "outside the walls," find solace at the Garden Tomb of Gordan's Calvary, a nineteenth-century alternative that continues to capture the imagination despite significant archaeological evidence dating that tomb to the Iron Age. However, as scholars we must remain committed to the evidence, even when it leads us away from established paths. It is in this spirit of rigorous inquiry that Todd M. West presents a compelling new case for a location that has, until now, remained hidden in plain sight: Bible Hill.

My own involvement with this research began somewhat serendipitously in the summer of 2023. While discussing the complex geography of first-century Jerusalem with Todd, I shared a realization that had been forming in my mind: the hillock popularly known today as Bible Hill, located in southwest Jerusalem, seemed to fit the Gospel accounts with startling precision. I suggested to Todd that this site deserved a formal, exhaustive investigation. I did not realize then that this initial spark would ignite a two-year obsession for the author. West took that suggestion and applied a level of due diligence that is rare in the field, testing the theory against the criteria of ancient texts, demography, and the physical remains of the Holy City. For two years, he bombarded my email inbox with what he correctly calls a "never-ending tsunami of evidence." This book is the result of that tireless labor. I can say with certainty that West's work represents a potential revolution in our understanding of biblical geography and understanding the "final week of Jesus."

It is important for me to state at the outset that my own scholarly work has led me to a different conclusion regarding the exact location of the crucifixion. For many years, I have argued, and continue to maintain, that the evidence most strongly supports a location on the Mount of Olives to the east. My view is rooted in the theological and topographical requirements found in the book of Hebrews regarding the *miphkad* altar and the ritual of the red heifer—as directly referenced in our earliest textual source: Hebrews 13:10–13. However, despite our differing conclusions, Todd West and I are in total agreement on one fundamental point: the traditional candidates are no longer viable. Like West, I do not accept the Church of the Holy Sepulcher as the historical site of Golgotha, nor do I believe the evidence supports Gordon's Calvary. By pointing Todd toward Bible Hill, I was challenging him to see if the western side of the city held a better alternative than the north or northwest traditions.

One of the most valuable aspects of this book is West's systematic deconstruction of the current candidates for Calvary. He notes that the traditional site at the Holy Sepulcher lacks documented criteria for its original verification in the fourth century. Furthermore, there is no definitive archaeological evidence that the site was actually outside the city walls in 30 CE; if it was inside, it fails the primary scriptural requirement that Jesus suffered "outside the gate." West also points to the high probability, supported by the writings of Josephus, that the location of the tomb area currently venerated as that of Jesus of Nazareth, belonged to the Jewish high priest John Hyrcanus (r. 134–104 BCE), the "George Washington" of Jewish independence under the Maccabees.

Similarly, Gordon's Calvary suffered a major blow when the famed archaeologist Dr. Gabriel Barkay confirmed that its "Garden Tomb" was hewn hundreds of years before the first century. The Gospels require a "new" rock-cut tomb dating to the time of the crucifixion. So, according to Scripture, the Garden Tomb of Gordon's Calvary cannot be the historical sepulcher of Jesus.

In contrast, Bible Hill fits both our textual, geographical, and archaeological evidence with remarkable consistency. The name "Golgotha" means "Skull" in Aramaic, and the Greek *kranion* can denote a "skullcap." Bible Hill, protruding from the Shoulder of Hinnom, looks remarkably like a giant skullcap sticking up out of the ground. Made of *meleke sultani* limestone—an extremely hard variety resistant to weathering—the hill likely retains the same cranial shape today that it possessed two thousand years ago. West provocatively connects this physical feature to the only "skull" explicitly linked with Jerusalem in the Hebrew Bible: Goliath's skull. He argues that David buried this trophy on the Shoulder of Hinnom, establishing a monument called the Place of the Skull that later served as a site for public executions.

The logistical case for Bible Hill is perhaps its most compelling feature. West follows the consensus of modern scholars who situate the Praetorium at Herod's Royal Palace on the western hill. From the palace's tribunal, excavated in the 1970s by Magen Broshi and Shimon Gibson, known as Gabbatha, Bible Hill sits only a third of a mile away. This creates a realistic "passion corridor" where Roman guards could securely escort prisoners out of the Judgment Gate and up the Road of the Patriarchs to a conspicuous execution site. This location allowed the Romans to satisfy their primary objective: using crucifixion as a public deterrent in front of the thousands of pilgrims streaming into the city from the south.

West's research uncovers "forensic" details that add layers of grit and reality to the narrative. He explores Cave 34 at Bible Hill, an Iron Age burial cave used through the Second Temple period where bodies were inexplicably left to decompose on top of one another—a practice unique in the Jerusalem necropolis. The discovery of a lead figurine of a decapitated man in this cave suggests

Bible Hill may have been Jerusalem's official "Place of Beheading" mentioned by St. Jerome. He even notes the presence of mulberry trees around the hill, suggesting the "sour wine" offered to Jesus might have been mulberry vinegar, which, unlike the "fruit of the vine," would have allowed Jesus to keep his vow made at the Last Supper to not drink of the vine until the kingdom came.

Furthermore, West offers a compelling re-reading of Easter Sunday. He argues that the traditional site makes the movements of the apostles—running through the heart of enemy territory near the Praetorium—patently absurd. Instead, he suggests the disciples were camping in the Rephaim Valley near Bible Hill, a common practice for Passover pilgrims. This proximity explains how Peter and John could have quickly reached the tomb and why the Roman guards' report to the chief priests at Caiaphas's mansion was logistically straightforward. The author even explores the *Toledot Yeshu*, a legendary rabbinic polemic against the resurrection which claims Jesus was buried by an aqueduct; West points out that several aqueducts existed on the Shoulder of Hinnom, providing a historical context for where such a rumor might have originated.

Beyond the logistics, the book delves into the deep typological and theological layers of the site. West connects Bible Hill to the Hill of God and the place where Abraham likely met Melchizedek. He explores the linguistic significance of the word "place" in Hebrew/Aramaic, showing that it can also mean "monument" as the modern "Place of the Name" (Yad Vashem/Holocaust Memorial) in Jerusalem demonstrates today. This suggests that when the Evangelists spoke of the "Place of the Skull," they may have been referring to a specific Davidic monument commemorating God's victory over Goliath. This connection transforms Golgotha from a random hill into a site of historical and national significance for the first-century Jewish mind.

As the one who first pointed Todd West toward this hill, I am deeply gratified to see the depth of research he has applied to it. He has not merely written a book; he has opened a conversation that bears further serious investigation. I encourage every reader—whether they be scholars, students, or pilgrims—to consider this new alternative with an open and critical mind. Todd West has provided the data; it is now up to us to weigh it. Whether you ultimately agree that Bible Hill is the historical Golgotha, you will find in these pages a wealth of archaeological and textual insight that demands to be taken seriously. This book is a vital contribution to the ongoing search for the historical Jesus and the world in which he lived and died.

Dr. James D. Tabor
Distinguished Fellow Humanities
Hebrew University
Retired Professor, UNC Charlotte

Preface

In the summer of 2023, while discussing the geography of Jerusalem with the renowned biblical scholar Dr. James D. Tabor, I realized he may have discovered the historical Calvary at a hillock popularly called Bible Hill in southwest Jerusalem. Because the geography and archaeology of Bible Hill seemed to fit the Gospel accounts, I decided to put Dr. Tabor's theory of Bible Hill as Golgotha to the test. Since the Church of the Holy Sepulcher, Gordon's Calvary, and Mount Olivet were already contenders for the place of Jesus' crucifixion when I started this investigation, I initially undertook due diligence by reviewing the evidence for each of them. None of the evidence convinced me that Jesus could have been crucified at any of these sites. So, I finally put Bible Hill to the test. The more evidence I uncovered, the stronger the case for Bible Hill as Golgotha became. What's more, every time I thought no more evidence could possibly be found, I was wrong. Within one or two days, more evidence would always come to light. Just ask Dr. Tabor. I bombarded his email inbox for over two years with the reams and reams of evidence I was collecting on Bible Hill. Moreover, there is only one rational explanation for this never-ending tsunami of evidence: Bible Hill must be the historical Calvary. This signals a potential revolution in our understanding of biblical geography. I will now present the results of my research, and allow you, the reader, to draw your own conclusions.

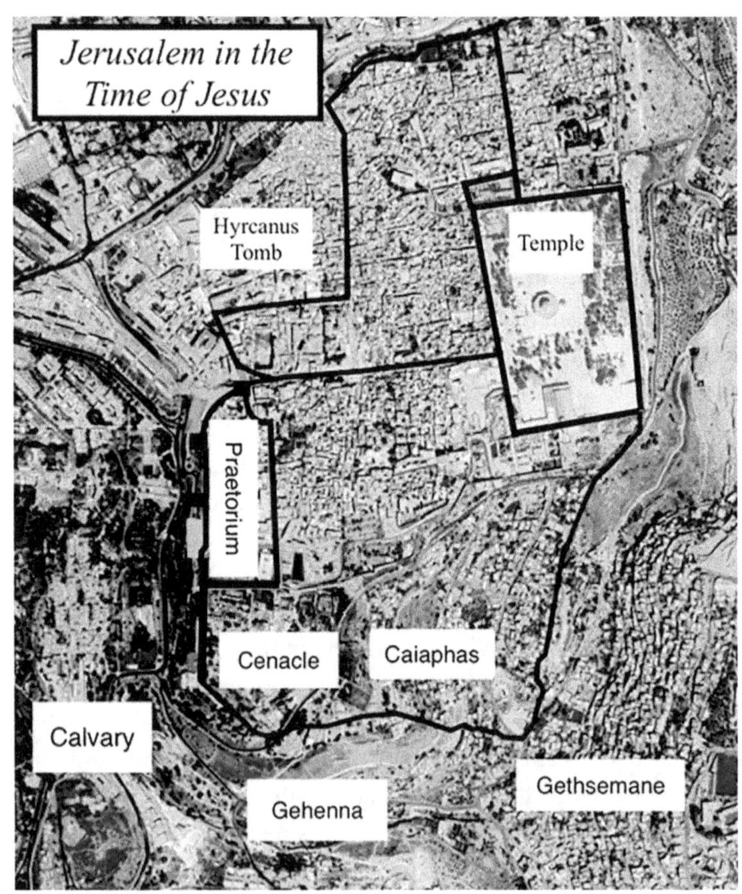

Photo from Google, Maxar Technologies. Imagery: 6/24/2012–newer.

1

Where Is Calvary?

The traditional Calvary at today's Church of the Holy Sepulcher was discovered in 326 CE by Queen Helena and Bishop Macarius under a temple of Venus built by the Roman emperor Hadrian in northwest Jerusalem.[1] The fact is, however, no one knows what criteria Helena and Macarius used to verify the authenticity of the traditional Calvary because the earliest records of its discovery do not share this information.[2] In that light, the alleged tomb of Christ in the Church of the Holy Sepulcher could have theoretically belonged to any affluent resident of the Holy City since the Iron Age. Likewise, because hundreds of crucifixions took place around the traditional Calvary during the Roman siege of Jerusalem in 70 CE, logic suggests the so-called true cross found by Helena under Hadrian's Temple of Venus was, in fact, a relic of war, not the cross used to crucify Jesus.[3] Thus, even the famous "true cross" does little to bolster the legitimacy of the traditional Calvary. In addition, despite nearly two centuries of archaeological research, there is currently no definitive evidence showing the traditional Calvary was even outside the walls of Jerusalem when

1. See Drijvers, "True Cross," 24–33; Joan Taylor, *Holy Places*, 113–14; and C. Wilson, *Holy Sepulchre*, 96–97.

2. C. Wilson, *Holy Sepulchre*, 9.

3. See Josephus, *War* 5.284–290.

Jesus was crucified.[4] This is noteworthy because Scripture states unequivocally that Jesus was crucified outside the city.[5] Even if the traditional Calvary was outside the walls in the time of Jesus, however, chances are good that the so-called tomb of Christ at the traditional Calvary originally belonged to the Jewish high priest John Hyrcanus, not Joseph of Arimathea.[6] To be certain, in 75 CE, the Jewish historian Josephus mentions the tomb of John Hyrcanus repeatedly in his descriptions of the area where Hadrian would later build his Temple of Venus in northwest Jerusalem, yet he never mentions anything about Golgotha or Joseph of Arimathea in these same descriptions even once.[7] Lastly, to bolster the case for the traditional Calvary, some scholars claim the authenticity of the traditional site only came into question in the nineteenth century as a result of "Scientific Protestantism."[8] This assertion is exaggerated. In the year 754, for instance, the Catholic bishop St. Willibald stated as a matter of fact that "[Calvary] was formerly outside Jerusalem; but Helena, when she found the [true cross], arranged that place so as to be within the city."[9] Then, in 1584, on his famous map of Jerusalem, the esteemed Catholic priest Fr. Christian van

4. See Avi-Yonah, "Walls," 122–25; Bahat, "Burial," 38–40; Cabaret, *Topography*, 11–26; Gibson, *Final Days*, loc. 40; Hanauer, "Controversy," 303; Herman, "Elusive Second Wall," 15:21; Ilmsens, "Penetrating Radar," paras. 1–15; Paton, "Third Wall," 199; Robinson and Smith, *Biblical Researches*, 463–64; Schein, "Second Wall of Jerusalem," 21–23; and C. Wilson, *Holy Sepulchre*, 124–37.

5. See, for instance, Heb 13:12.

6. See Martin, *Secrets*, 260; Tabor, *Lost Mary*, 73–74; and C. Wilson, *Holy Sepulchre*, 96, 100.

7. Josephus knew many things about Jesus of Nazareth, including the reports of Jesus' resurrection from the dead. He probably learned about Jesus from Ananus II (who killed James the Just [who wrote the Epistle of James]) because Ananus II was Josephus's commanding officer in the First Jewish-Roman War. Josephus could have learned about Jesus from Herod Agrippa II as well. This is because Josephus was on speaking terms with Herod Agrippa II (who was himself on speaking terms with the apostle Paul). See Acts 26:28; Josephus, *Antiquities* 18.63–64, 20.200; Schmidt, *Josephus and Jesus*, 145, 187–90, 255; and Tabor, *Jesus Dynasty*, 226.

8. See Kochav, "Search," 278–83.

9. Willibald, *Hodoeporicon*, 19.

Adrichem placed the tomb of John Hyrcanus at the traditional Calvary and put Golgotha north of the Damascus Gate.[10] About a century after that, in his description of Jerusalem, the Anglican priest Thomas Fuller also rejected the traditional Calvary, locating the crucifixion of Jesus hundreds of yards west of the Church of the Holy Sepulcher.[11] Next, in 1738, the German pilgrim Jonas Korte even wrote an entire book attacking the authenticity of the traditional site of Golgotha.[12] All this demonstrates that "there has long been more than one view regarding the site of Calvary and that the traditional site was by no means [left] unchallenged [before the 1800s]."[13]

When Gordon's Calvary was identified in the nineteenth century as a plausible location for the historical Golgotha, it was celebrated by Protestants all over the world as a rational alternative to the traditional Calvary.[14] For one, unlike the traditional site of Golgotha, Gordon's Calvary was unquestionably outside the walls of Jerusalem in the time of Jesus, and it seemed to meet all the other prerequisites needed to be Golgotha as well.[15] Plus, according to one tradition, Gordon's Calvary was Jerusalem's "Place of Stoning" in the first century, correlating the site with public executions in antiquity.[16] The hill of Gordon's Calvary also looked like a giant skull, complementing the Gospel of Luke in which Golgotha is simply called the "Skull." In 1986, however, the apparent strength of Gordon's Calvary suffered a major blow. Research by the famed archaeologist Dr. Gabriel Barkay confirmed that the alleged tomb of Christ at Gordon's Calvary was hewn hundreds of years before the first century.[17] This was a serious setback for Gordon's Calvary

10. See Crawley-Boevey, "Van Adrichem," 64–68.

11. Fuller, *Bisgah*, 297.

12. See C. Wilson, *Holy Sepulchre*, 45.

13. Crawley-Boevey, "Recent Opinions," 26.

14. See J. Chadwick, "Revisiting Golgotha," 13–48; Howe, *True Site*, 20; McBirnie, *Authentic Tomb*, 40–53; and C. Wilson, *Holy Sepulchre*, 114–15.

15. See Crawley-Boevey, "Golgotha and the Holy Sepulchre," 270.

16. Hanauer, "Place of Stoning," 319.

17. Barkay, "Garden Tomb," 52.

because the tomb in which Jesus was laid to rest at Golgotha cannot predate the eighteenth year of the reign of Tiberius Caesar around 30 CE.[18] It is also apparent now that Gordon's Calvary is susceptible to erosion, undermining the premise that it looked like a skull in the time of Jesus.[19] Moreover, because archaeological evidence indicates Jesus was tried nearly a mile away from Gordon's Calvary, it is unlikely that Pilate would have transported Jesus (and two other prisoners) all the way there through the crowded, volatile streets of northwest Jerusalem to be crucified.[20]

A third candidate for Calvary is the "miphkad altar" on Mount Olivet where red heifers were ritually sacrificed in the first century for the cleansing of sin.[21] According to advocates of this site, the gate facing Calvary mentioned in the Epistle to the Hebrews is none other than the main eastern gate of the Temple that faced the miphkad altar on Mount Olivet.[22] If this is correct, then logic suggests Calvary was located somewhere close to the miphkad altar. It would also signify that Jesus died like a red heifer near the miphkad altar to purify the people of their sins. While this prospect is admittedly intriguing, it is not very plausible. Jesus is frequently called the Passover Lamb, for instance, yet he was not crucified in the Temple. So, even though Jesus is compared to a red heifer in Hebrews, this does not mean he necessarily died at the miphkad altar on Mount Olivet. Additionally, archaeological evidence indicates the trial of Jesus took place over a mile away from the miphkad altar.[23] In that light, if Jesus was crucified by the miphkad altar, he would have walked over a mile from the Praetorium through the potentially riotous streets of Jerusalem,

18. See C. Wilson, *Holy Sepulchre*, 34.

19. See Bolen, "Nose," para. 3; Colon, "Gordon's Calvary," para. 7; and C. Wilson, *Holy Sepulchre*, 115–16.

20. See Edwards et al., "Physical Death," 1455–63; Gibson, "Trial of Jesus," 108–118; Lemonon, *Pilate et le Gouvernement*, 117–24; and Magness, *Holy Land*, 158–59.

21. See Cornuke, *Golgotha*, 182; Hutchinson, "Notes," 379–81; Manning, *Holy Fields*, 106–7; Martin, *Secrets*, 9–32; and Tabor, *Jesus Dynasty*, 226.

22. See Heb 13:12; and Martin, *Secrets*, 9–32.

23. See Magness, *Holy Land*, 158–59.

across the Kidron Valley, and up the steep slope of Mount Olivet to be crucified. This scenario is doubtful on both security and logistical grounds. What's more, because Mount Olivet is seemingly always identified by name in the Gospels whenever a significant event occurs there, logic suggests, if Jesus had been crucified on Mount Olivet near the miphkad altar, at least one of the Evangelists would have pointed this detail out. Furthermore, according to the translation of Heb 13:12 in the ancient Peshitta Bible (ca. 400 CE), Jesus was crucified outside "the city," not outside "the gate." This is notable because it undercuts the idea that the gate cited in Heb 13:12 must be an allusion to the eastern gate of the Temple.[24] This in turn undermines the very foundation of the miphkad altar theory of Calvary.

24. As one of the oldest translations of the Greek New Testament in existence, the Peshitta Bible aids modern scholars in understanding how the earliest Christians interpreted the original Greek versions of the New Testament.

2

Bible Hill as Calvary: An Introduction

Bible Hill looks like a giant skullcap protruding high above the Shoulder of Hinnom in southwest Jerusalem.[1] It makes two cameos in the book of Joshua as a boundary marker between the tribes of Benjamin and Judah.[2] Plus, everyone in the Bible who ever came to Jerusalem, including Abraham, Rachel, David, Mary, Joseph, and Jesus, at one time or another, gazed at Bible Hill.[3] At some point in the late seventh century BCE, a resplendent cemetery of opulent limestone tombs was hewn along the northern slope of Bible Hill. These tombs were truly regal, indicating the presence of Judean nobility.[4] Indeed, according to the renowned archaeologist Zeev Erlich, they were hewn in the Garden of Uzza where the notorious Davidic monarchs Manasseh and Amon were

1. As a technical term, the "Shoulder of Hinnom" refers to the precipitous rock escarpment just below Bible Hill facing the Hinnom Valley (see Barkay, *Ketef Hinnom*, 10). In other words, it is the southwest corner of the longer "Shoulder of Jerusalem" (see Josh 15:8). However, in this book, it also denotes Bible Hill and the area immediately surrounding Bible Hill, including today's First Station Shopping Center and the Mount Zion Hotel.

2. Bible Hill seems to make a cameo in the book of First Enoch as well (see 1 En. 26:4).

3. See Barkay, *Ketef Hinnom*, 10.

4. Barkay, *Ketef Hinnom*, 20.

entombed.[5] This is noteworthy because, if Erlich is correct (and if Bible Hill is Calvary), it means Jesus was interred in a royal garden near two of the most infamous Davidic kings in history, giving new meaning to Isaiah's prophecy that the Messiah would be assigned a grave with the wicked and with the rich, though he had done no violence.[6]

Given its strategic location and imposing height above the Hinnom Valley, it is truly astonishing how the historical record goes virtually silent on Bible Hill following the book of Joshua.[7] Ironically, this very silence boosts the odds of Bible Hill being Golgotha because it means nothing in the historical record precludes Bible Hill from being the site of Jesus' crucifixion. That Bible Hill could be Calvary is not an implausible assumption either. Certainly, writing over a century ago (before the ruins of Pilate's tribunal on Mount Zion had been excavated), the esteemed biblical scholar Dr. Theodore Keim suggested that "[Calvary] probably lay on the south-west of [Jerusalem] . . . [by] the Palace of Pilate . . . in the southern Valley of the Sons of Hinnom, . . . [where] the descent into the valley . . . might have easily presented a hilly contour in which the popular fancy saw a resemblance to a skull."[8] Also writing over a century ago without the aid of today's archaeological discoveries to shield her from criticism, Dr. Mary Brodrick nevertheless stated as a matter of fact that "though most writers place [Calvary] on the north side of [Jerusalem], there is no reason why it should not have been on the south[west] side."[9]

5. Erlich, "Garden of Uzza," 61–79.

6. See Isa 53:9 and Matt 27:57.

7. Even the origin of its modern name "Bible Hill" is a mystery. It may stem from a proposal in the 1960s by the Israel Society for Biblical Research to build a center for biblical studies at Bible Hill. Others say the name comes from the simple fact that Bible Hill is mentioned in the Bible (see Dunlop, *Faith Rewarded*, 64). The local name for Bible Hill is "Squill Hill" because so many squills grow there each summer.

8. Keim, *Jesus of Nazara*, 134–35. See also Haupt, "Golgotha," 240.

9. Brodrick, *Trial and Crucifixion*, 137. It is also noteworthy that, in 1979, the oldest biblical texts ever found on earth were excavated on Bible Hill (see Barkay, *Ketef Hinnom*, 34). The texts were inscribed on tiny silver scrolls that date back to the time of the prophet Jeremiah (ca. 600 BCE).

Bible Hill as Golgotha[10]

10. "Vallée de Gihon et l'Etang Inferieur," photo by Felix Bonfils, 1870–79. National Library of Israel, Lenkin Family Photograph Collection, University of Pennsylvania Library, Pritzker Family National Photograph Collection. Public domain.

3

The Skull

EVIDENCE SUGGESTS THE SITE where Jesus was crucified looked like a skull, skullcap, or head. To be sure, the name Golgotha means "skull" in Aramaic. Moreover, according to the Gospel of Luke, Golgotha was also called *kranion*, a word which means skull or skullcap in Greek.[1] Plus, in all the extant Old Syriac Gospels (ca. 200 CE), Golgotha is always referred to as the Skull, never the Place of the Skull.[2] Also, according to the ancient Christian theologian Pseudo-Tertullian (writing ca. 250 CE), Golgotha means the skull-pan of the head.[3] In Codex Sinaiticus (ca. 350 CE), Calvary is called *the Golgotha*, which literally means the Skull.[4] Finally, in

1. Beekes, *Etymological Dictionary*, 770.

2. See Haelewyck, "Old Syriac," 146; and Lewis, *Syriac of the Sinaitic*, 56, 92, 159.

3. See Pseudo-Tertullian, "Harmony," 341.

4. See Mark 15:22 in Codex Sinaiticus. It is also noteworthy that the earliest possible reference to Calvary as a "hill" or "mountain" may be hidden in plain sight in the Shem-Tob Hebrew Gospel of Matthew. According to Shem Tob's Matthew, Jesus was crucified at "*Gulgota*, that is, *Har Calvary*" (see Howard, *Hebrew Gospel*, 145). If the original Hebrew underlying *Har Calvary* was *Har Gulgota*, it would boost the odds that the historical Golgotha was a large hillock like Bible Hill. This premise is reinforced by the Bordeaux Pilgrim (333 CE) who called Calvary the "Hill of Golgotha" possibly because he was a Judeo-Christian paraphrasing the original Hebrew Gospel of Matthew (see

the Peshitta Bible (ca. 400 CE), Calvary is always called either the Skull or the Head, but never the Place of the Skull or the Place of the Head.

Scholars who utilize the ancient descriptions of Calvary as a skull, skullcap, or head to formulate theories of Calvary's location usually suggest the crucifixion of Jesus took place on a bald knoll or a skull-shaped hill somewhere on the outskirts of Jerusalem.[5] These scholars also frequently associate Golgotha with prominence and wide visibility.[6] Lord Bishop Jeremy Taylor, for instance, says, "Calvary, a place difficult in the ascent, eminent and apt for the publication of shame, a hill of death and dead bones."[7] The renowned biblical scholar Ernst Renan likewise asserts that "Golgotha . . . probably designates a smooth hill, having the form of a bald skull."[8]

It so happens Bible Hill looks like a giant skullcap sticking up out of the ground.[9] Indeed, according to the book of Joshua, Bible Hill is both the "head" and the "face" over the "shoulder" of Jerusalem.[10] While any summit may be called a head in Hebrew, the description of Bible Hill in the book of Joshua is a clear allusion to the head of a human being sitting over his or her shoulder. This assertion is reinforced by the traditional Arabic name for Bible Hill—Ras al Dabus—because, in Arabic, *ras* often denotes hills that rise up out of the ground like heads.[11] Bible Hill is also made of *meleke sultani*, one of the hardest varieties of limestone,

---

Pixner, *Messiah*, 343; and Tabor, "Locating Golgotha," para. 12).

5. See J. Chadwick, "Revisiting Golgotha," 22.

6. C. Wilson, *Holy Sepulchre*, 11.

7. Jeremy Taylor, *Whole Works*, 337.

8. Renan, *Life of Jesus*, 344.

9. It rises about half a mile above the valley bed (see Barkay, *Ketef Hinnom*, 10).

10. See Josh 15:8.

11. Joan Taylor, "Golgotha," para. 4. See also Barkay, *Ketef Hinnom*, 10; Gibson, *Final Days*, loc. 117; and Schick, "Boundary," 185. *Ras al Dabus* means "head of the pin" or "head of the femur bone."

which is extremely resistant to weathering.[12] This is significant because it boosts the probability that the cranial shape of Bible Hill today reflects what Bible Hill looked like two thousand years ago, increasing the chances that Bible Hill was called "Golgotha" in the time of Jesus. By contrast, "there is . . . no surviving feature of the Holy Sepulcher's 'Hill of Calvary' that can be identified in any way with a skull, nor is any such feature mentioned in the account of [its discovery by Queen Helena and Bishop Macarius]."[13]

As a side note, in the time of Jesus, the northeastern slope of Bible Hill served as a quarry.[14] This is notable because, as the renowned biblical scholar Dr. Joan Taylor explains, "if in the slanting light of the morning and evening, the shape of . . . the rocks and caves [of a quarry] started to take on the appearance of a skull, or a human head, perhaps we have a reason for the location [of Golgotha] being called 'the skull place.'"[15] While Dr. Taylor was referring to the quarry under the Church of the Holy Sepulcher in the above quote, her statement's veracity would nevertheless also apply to the first-century quarry on the northeastern slope of Bible Hill.[16] What's more, if the quarry at Bible Hill did cause Bible Hill's northeastern slope to look like the face of a giant skull, it would have totally dwarfed Gordon's Calvary by comparison. This of course boosts the odds even more that Bible Hill could have been called Golgotha in the time of Jesus. It is also worth mentioning that the hard limestone of Bible Hill would have been perfect for drilling deep, permanent postholes for the stipes of large Latin-style crosses. This is relevant to Bible Hill as Calvary because it proves every type of cross, from the biggest to the smallest, could have been erected over the Shoulder of Hinnom to intimidate onlookers from as far away as Mount Olivet when Jesus was crucified. It also proves that an elevated line of Latin-style crosses could have

12. See Gill, "Bedrock," 220.
13. J. Chadwick, "Revisiting Golgotha," 20.
14. Barkay, *Ketef Hinnom*, 18.
15. Joan Taylor, "Golgotha," para. 9.
16. See Avner and Zelinger, "Cemetery," 27.

been erected where St. Andrew's Memorial Church sits on Bible Hill today, striking immeasurable fear into the populace.[17]

Remnants of the First-Century Quarry at Bible Hill[18]

17. St. Andrew's Memorial Church was built on the northern slope of Bible Hill in 1930 as a memorial to Scottish soldiers who were killed in Palestine during the First World War.

18. "Ketef Hinnom," photo by Todd Bolen, Bible Places, Sept. 2, 1999. Used with permission.

4

Place of Crucifixion

IRON NAILS HAVE BEEN found in the burial urns of Roman soldiers on Bible Hill.[1] This is salient because these nails may have been used in crucifixions.[2] To be certain, in antiquity, crucifixion nails were viewed as extremely powerful magical amulets that could help people in both this life and the next.[3] Indeed, according to the Roman naturalist Pliny the Elder (writing in 70 CE), in his day, crucifixion nails were coveted for their healing properties.[4] Likewise, the distinguished poet Lucan (writing in 65 CE) confirms that witches in antiquity craved crucifixion nails to use in their magic.[5] Even the ancient Jews sought out crucifixion nails for their apparent paranormal powers.[6] It should come as no surprise then that "immediately after crucified victims were cut down from their crosses, the nails [were] removed from their bodies and pocketed."[7] The Gospel of Peter (ca. 150 CE) is illustrative in this

1. Barkay, "Riches of Ketef Hinnom," 26–27.

2. See Lidz, "Dead Nails," para 1.

3. See Claeys et al., "Magical Practices," 158; Lidz, "Dead Nails," para. 1; and Robinson, "Crucifixion," 33.

4. Robinson, "Crucifixion," 43.

5. Lucan, *Civil War*, 543–47.

6. M. Sabb. 6:10.

7. Roberts, "Miracles," para. 90.

regard, as it narrates how the executioners at Golgotha purloined the nails from the hands of Jesus after he was taken down from the cross.[8] In light of the above, the iron nails found on Bible Hill in the Roman burial urns boost the odds that crucifixions occurred on the Shoulder of Hinnom in antiquity.[9] This, in turn, reinforces the premise that Bible Hill is Golgotha. What's more, in a tomb just south of Bible Hill, archaeologists found two iron nails in the ossuary of the high priest Caiaphas (i.e., the high priest who handed Jesus over to Pilate to be crucified).[10] In the opinion of some scholars, these nails were used to crucify someone such as Jesus.[11] If this is accurate, then the proximity of Bible Hill to the tomb of Caiaphas could be telling. It is also notable that four iron nails were ritualistically positioned by the charred bones of a Hellenistic-era courtesan just south of Bible Hill in Ramat Rahel.[12] Given that the Greeks crucified people since the time of Alexander the Great, the four iron nails in this tomb could be the first ever crucifixion nails from Bible Hill.[13]

In the Roman Empire of the first century, crucified victims were typically left on the cross to suffer for days, and their bodies would remain hanging on the cross to rot or be eaten by animals.[14] However, to comply with Mosaic law, Jews could not leave anyone hanging on a cross overnight as the Romans did, or allow a corpse

8. As one of the earliest Christian texts outside the New Testament, the Gospel of Peter is useful in the interpretation of Scripture because it provides valuable insights into the most ancient of Christian beliefs and traditions.

9. The exact size of the nails in the Roman burial urns on Bible Hill is not cited anywhere in the available literature. The literature only says they were small (see Barkay, "Riches of Ketef Hinnom," 27). Since crucifixion nails for the hands could be as short as two inches, the fact that the nails in the burial urns from Bible Hill are called small does not preclude them from having been used in crucifixions (see Franz, "Nails from Caiaphas' Tomb," para. 12; and the illustration in David, "Nails," after para. 13).

10. Windle, "Caiaphas," para. 13.

11. See Shimron et al., "Petrochemistry," 260.

12. Steinmeyer, "Hetaira," para. 2.

13. Future researchers should test all the nails around Bible Hill for DNA.

14. See Crossan, *Jesus*, 174.

to remain on the cross unburied after sunset. So, at least in Palestine, Jews insisted that people who were crucified be also dead and buried on the same day as their execution.[15] Thus, while not mandatory, it would have been prudent (to avoid unnecessary riots) for Roman governors in Palestine to have (at minimum) killed and dumped crucified criminals in pit graves before sunset.[16] This would certainly explain why Pilate, despite typical Roman crucifixion practice, readily agreed to break the legs of Jesus and the brigands to kill them before nightfall.[17] It would also suggest that the pit graves excavated on the northern slope of Bible Hill could be the final resting place of the two brigands who were crucified with Jesus.[18] The coins minted by Pontius Pilate that were found in and around these pit graves buttress this contention.[19]

Bible Hill also fits the description of a typical Roman site of crucifixion. Indeed, in the words of the Roman educator Quintilian (writing in 95 CE), "when [Romans] crucify criminals, the most frequented roads are chosen, where the greatest number of people can look and be seized by fear."[20] The preeminent army officer and historian Major-General Charles Wilson sustains Quintilian's description, saying, "The Romans crucified criminals outside the city or camp. They usually selected for such executions the side of a frequented road or pathway; but they often carried them out in a conspicuous place . . . set apart for the purpose . . . [and] occasionally on a hill."[21] Clearly then, Bible Hill has the prerequisites needed to be a Roman place of crucifixion, from its prominent position just outside Jerusalem to its location along the famous

15. See Deut 21:22; and Josephus, *War* 4.317.

16. See Barkay, *Ketef Hinnom*, 18.

17. See John 19:31–32.

18. See Grass, *Ostergeschehen*, 179–80.

19. See Barkay, *Ketef Hinnom*, 18. It is relevant that coins minted by the Roman governors Valerius-Gratus (r. ca. 15–26 CE) and Coponius (r. ca. 6–9 CE) have been excavated in these pit graves as well (see Barkay, *Ketef Hinnom*, 18).

20. Quintilian, *Lesser Declamations*, 1:259.

21. C. Wilson, *Holy Sepulchre*, 22.

Road of the Patriarchs. This in turn bolsters the premise that Bible Hill is Calvary.

As a side note, Bible Hill is also a site where Jesus could have been crucified on a living tree—as the trees near the summit of Bible Hill today confirm. This is noteworthy because Scripture says five times that Jesus was crucified on a tree.[22] Moreover, a number of prominent scholars have interpreted these five verses literally.[23] With that in mind, the fact that Bible Hill is where Jesus could have been crucified on a living tree underpins the assertion that Bible Hill is Golgotha.

22. See Acts 5:30, 10:39, 13:29; Gal 3:13; and 1 Pet 2:24.

23. See, for instance, Martin, *Secrets*, 290–303; and I. Wilson, *Murder at Golgotha*, loc. 81.

5

The Place of Beheading

According to the famous theologian St. Jerome (writing in 398 CE), there were places outside Jerusalem in his day where the heads of condemned criminals were cut off, and, for this reason, they were each called Calvary.[1] With that in mind, Jerome concluded that Jesus had been crucified at a place where criminals were routinely beheaded.[2] This is relevant to Bible Hill as Golgotha because Bible Hill appears to have been Jerusalem's official "Place of Beheading" in the time of Jesus. Consider the following evidence.

As suggested in the Babylonian and Jerusalem Talmuds, during the Second Temple period, certain criminals in Jerusalem were put to death either at the "Place of Burning and Stoning" or the "Place of Beheading and Strangulation."[3] According to some authorities, there was a cave near the Place of Beheading and Strangulation wherein the executioners would place the heads and

1. See C. Wilson, *Holy Sepulchre*, 21–22.

2. See C. Wilson, *Holy Sepulchre*, 7.

3. See Gibson, *Final Days*, loc. 131; Warren, "Golgotha," 226; and C. Wilson, *Holy Sepulchre*, 10. The "Place of Beheading and Strangulation" is never mentioned specifically in the Talmud. Its existence is inferred from the fact that criminals who were beheaded or strangled were buried at a separate site from those who were stoned or burned.

bodies of the condemned to decompose.[4] This is notable because one of the Iron Age burial caves at Bible Hill (i.e., Cave 34) not only was used continuously during the Second Temple period, but every generation who used Cave 34 would inexplicably let new bodies decompose on top of earlier layers of bones in the cave.[5] At the time of its discovery, "no prior example" of such a burial cave had ever been found anywhere else around Jerusalem.[6] Additionally, a lead figurine of a *decapitated and bound nude male* was found in Cave 34 dating to the Second Temple period.[7] The figurine clearly shows a decapitated man with his hands tied behind his back. A glass pendant of a grotesque human head was also discovered in Cave 34.[8] If Bible Hill is the Place of Beheading, these items could be indicative of the role Cave 34 played in public beheadings in Jerusalem in antiquity. In any event, pursuant to the Talmud of Jerusalem, if someone had a relative who was beheaded or strangled by court order, he or she could retrieve the bones of that relative from the execution site once the flesh on the bones had decomposed.[9] If this is accurate (and if Cave 34 is the cave where the bodies of beheaded and strangled victims were placed in Jerusalem in the Second Temple period), it would explain why excavations of Cave 34 did not find piles of decapitated skulls inside. Additionally, because the hyoid bone is frequently left unfractured in cases of violent strangulation, it is no surprise that investigators never detected any evidence of strangulation in the skeletal remains of Cave 34 either.[10]

It is worth noting that if Cave 34 was the public repository for beheaded and strangled criminals in Jerusalem, then the head of James Zebedee may have rested there after Herod Agrippa

4. See C. Wilson, *Holy Sepulchre*, 7.

5. See Barkay, "Riches of Ketef Hinnom," 27. Cave 34 is located behind today's Menachem Begin Heritage Center.

6. Barkay, *Ketef Hinnom*, 15.

7. See Barkay, *Ketef Hinnom*, 17; and Kloner and Zissu, *Necropolis*, 362.

8. See Barkay, *Ketef Hinnom*, 22.

9. See C. Wilson, *Holy Sepulchre*, 7.

10. See Pollanen and Chiasson, "Fracture," 110–13.

chopped it off in 44 CE.[11] Perhaps the head of James Zebedee's jailer ended up in Cave 34 as well because, according to Eusebius (writing in 330 CE), Herod Agrippa beheaded him for confessing Jesus as Lord during James Zebedee's trial.[12] Because tradition says the apostle Matthias (who replaced Judas Iscariot among the twelve apostles) was beheaded in Jerusalem, his head may have been placed in Cave 34 as well.[13] It may also be assumed that Peter's head would have wound up in Cave 34, had he not escaped Jerusalem before Herod Agrippa could execute him.[14] While Peter avoided execution, his prison guards were not so lucky, as Agrippa executed them for losing Peter.[15] If Agrippa had them decapitated, it is possible that their heads were placed in Cave 34 as well. Lending credence to this speculation is the coin of Herod Agrippa (r. 41–44 CE) that was excavated in Cave 34.[16]

As a side note (if Bible Hill is the Place of Beheading and Strangulation), it would be logical to assume that the enigmatic layers of bones found in Cave 34 were the skeletal remains of victims that were never retrieved by relatives. It is also conceivable that the pit graves on the northern slope of Bible Hill were reserved for crucifixion victims. This system would have helped relatives know where to collect the bones of their loved ones.

11. See Acts 12:1–2.
12. See Silver, *House of Herod*, 112.
13. See Jacquier, "St. Matthias," para. 2.
14. See Acts 12:4–11.
15. See Acts 12:19.
16. See Kloner and Zissu, *Necropolis*, 362.

6

The Roots of the Place of Beheading

In the sixth century BCE, the prophet Jeremiah bashed the people of Jerusalem, calling them liars, murderers, adulterers, and worshipers of false gods.[1] Then he prophesied that, in the coming Babylonian siege (587 BCE), the Hinnom Valley would come to be called "Slaughter Valley" because so many Jerusalemites would die and be piled up there (due to their abominations).[2] Jeremiah also prophesied the Babylonians would scatter the bones of Jerusalem's kings, princes, priests, and prophets on the places where the people of Jerusalem worshiped the sun, moon, stars, and other false gods.[3] While no one knows for certain where the events of these prophecies took place, evidence suggests it could have occurred around Bible Hill. To be sure, consider the following evidence:

1. According to Scripture, in the years leading up to the Babylonian siege, King Manasseh and King Amon worshiped false gods and sacrificed children around Jerusalem. King Manasseh even sacrificed his own sons in the Hinnom Valley.[4] It so happens, in one of the Iron Age bone-pits excavated

1. See Jer 7:1–16.
2. See Jer 7:32–34.
3. See Jer 8:1–3.
4. See 2 Chr 33:1–20.

on Bible Hill, about 40 percent of the bones excavated there belonged to children under nine years of age.[5] What's more, the skeletal remains of infants less than a year old made up the single largest group of bones by age at death found in the grave. Plus, the archaeologist who excavated the infant bones asserted they were almost certainly found *in situ*. Since Scripture says King Manasseh and King Amon sacrificed children around Jerusalem, including the Hinnom Valley—it is not inconceivable that the bones of the Iron Age children excavated on Bible Hill constitute hard evidence for child sacrifice having taken place at this location in the time of Jeremiah, the very type of abomination Jeremiah railed against.

2. Two miles south of Bible Hill (in today's district of Ramat Rahel) a royal palace from the time of King Manasseh and King Amon was excavated in 1931, and the identity of this site as a royal palace of the Judahite kings has been confirmed by multiple additional excavations since then.[6] A government complex from the time of Manasseh has also been excavated at Ramat Rahel.[7] This is salient because it boosts the probability that King Manasseh and King Amon spent significant time on the Shoulder of Hinnom, which in turn boosts the odds that the children found in the bone-pit on Bible Hill are the victims of child sacrifice at the hands of these two kings. This in turn indicates the northern slope of Bible Hill was the sort of place where Jeremiah's prophecies would have occurred.

3. Arrowheads from the Babylonian siege were excavated on Bible Hill, indicating the Babylonians were at Bible Hill in 587 BCE to carry out Jeremiah's prophecies, like throwing dead bodies from the Shoulder of Hinnom into Slaughter Valley and callously scattering the bones of Jerusalem's kings,

5. See Nagar, "Skeletal Remains," 55.
6. See Barkay, "Royal Palace," 34.
7. Windle, "Administrative Complex," para. 1.

> princes, and prophetic priests all around the Garden of Uzza.[8] (The burial of Jehoiada in the City of David confirms that high priests could be entombed in royal cemeteries such as the Garden of Uzza.)

If Bible Hill was the place where the events of Jeremiah's prophecies took place, then the northern slope of Bible Hill would have been totally defiled following the Babylonian siege of Jerusalem. It would have been rational then for later residents of Jerusalem to have turned this sullied area of the Shoulder of Hinnom into a permanent place for criminal executions, especially if King David buried Goliath's decapitated skull at Bible Hill when he brought it to Jerusalem as recorded in Scripture.[9] After all, if David buried Goliath's skull on the Shoulder of Hinnom, it would have been a brilliant idea to transform the sullied northern slope of Bible Hill into the official Place of Beheading—where the skulls of new enemies of Israel could join Goliath's.

8. See Barkay, *Ketef Hinnom*, 22–24.

9. See 1 Sam 17:4.

7

Goliath's Skull

THE OLDEST AND MOST venerated tradition about Calvary says that Adam's skull was buried there and Jesus was crucified on top of it.[1] This is puzzling to say the least. After all, there is no account of Adam's skull anywhere in the Bible. By contrast, Goliath's skull not only appears in Scripture but also constitutes the one and only skull in the entire Hebrew Bible explicitly linked with Jerusalem.[2] What's more, after David beheaded Goliath in the Elah Valley and took the giant's skull to the Holy City, he must have immediately buried it somewhere nearby because (according to the Hebrew Bible, Greek Septuagint, Targum Jonathan, Peshitta Bible, and Latin Vulgate) the Holy City was the last place Goliath's skull ever saw the light of day.[3] In addition, recent excavations provide compelling evidence that the Israelites and Philistines did fight each other in the Elah Valley as Scripture attests. This bolsters the historicity of the biblical account describing David taking Goliath's skull to

1. See C. Wilson, *Holy Sepulchre*, 2.

2. The skull of the Syrian-Greek general Nicanor was brought to Jerusalem by Judas Maccabeus in 161 BCE according to both 1 and 2 Maccabees. The severed head of the pseudo-messiah Theudas was brought to Jerusalem by Roman soldiers in 45 CE (see Josephus, *Antiquities* 20.97–99).

3. See Hertzberg, *I and II Samuel*, 153.

Jerusalem.[4] Clearly then, Goliath's skull is a much stronger candidate for the skull of Golgotha than the skull of Adam.

While the Bible never reveals what route David took to reach Jerusalem with his freshly beheaded prize, the Road of the Patriarchs is a safe bet. If he took this road, he would have walked by his hometown of Bethlehem, where he could rest and resupply. This would explain why Scripture says David put Goliath's armor in his "tent" as he made his way to Jerusalem with Goliath's skull ("tent" is a synonym for "hometown" in biblical Hebrew).[5] Scripture also suggests David did not dally in Bethlehem. So, after recouping his strength, he must have immediately walked to Jerusalem to taunt his Jebusite enemies with the head of Goliath; when David killed Goliath, the Holy City was ruled by enemies of Israel called Jebusites. Since the Road of the Patriarchs leads straight to the Shoulder of Hinnom, it makes sense that David would have confronted the Jebusites from Bible Hill. Indeed, for David to have approached Jerusalem any closer would have been tantamount to suicide. This is because the Jebusites were fierce and would have killed David instantly if he had walked through the Hinnom Valley brandishing Goliath's skull before them like an arrogant fool. However, evidence indicates the area around Bible Hill was not occupied by the Jebusites when David killed Goliath.[6] As a result, the future king of Israel would have been relatively safe provoking his enemies down in the Hinnom Valley from atop Bible Hill.[7] Plus, according to some scholars, David may have dedicated Goliath's sword to God at a town just three miles north of Bible Hill.[8] If this is correct, the proximity of Goliath's sword to Bible Hill lends even more credence to the premise that David buried Goliath's skull on the Shoulder of Hinnom. What's more, a few years after taking Goliath's skull to Jerusalem, David brandished the royal spear of King Saul while taunting the commander of King Saul's army

4. Ngo, "Biblical Sha'arayim," paras. 1–5.

5. See Hoffmeier, "David's Triumph," 97.

6. See Josephus, *Antiquities* 5.136–140, 7.65–68; and Judg 19:12.

7. See Barkay, *Ketef Hinnom*, 10.

8. See Barkay et al., "Iron Age Fortress," 66.

from across a valley while standing on the summit of a high hill.[9] This proves David could have (and plausibly would have) done the same thing with Goliath's skull on the Shoulder of Hinnom.

While the Bible never reveals the motives driving David to bring Goliath's skull to Jerusalem, logic suggests they would have been strategic in nature.[10] For instance, although Goliath was not a Jebusite, his reputation as a ferocious fighter would have nevertheless been well known in Jerusalem. So, seeing Goliath's bloody head on a stake would have shocked and struck fear into David's Jebusite enemies. Plus, when David beheaded Goliath, Bible Hill also lay before the territory of David's other sworn enemy—the Philistines—who frequently raided the Rephaim Valley to the southwest of the Shoulder of Hinnom. As a result, when David brought Goliath's skull to Jerusalem, the future king of Israel was likely taking the first step in turning Bible Hill into a symbol of God's supremacy. In short, after conquering Jerusalem, David would build a monument to God on Bible Hill, commemorating the defeat of Goliath. Its name would be the Place of the Skull.[11] Then every Philistine who approached the new City of David would recall that a lowly shepherd slew their greatest warrior because the God of Israel reigns supreme. If this is accurate, it would certainly explain why the Philistines repeatedly attacked Jerusalem from a weak position on the Shoulder of Hinnom after David defeated the Jebusites.[12] Put simply, the Philistines were probably prowling around Bible Hill because they wanted to recover Goliath's skull. It is also notable that, according to Scripture, the Rephaim Valley was named after an ancient tribe of giants who hated Israel and were the ancestors of Goliath.[13] In that light, the fact that Bible Hill faces the valley named after Goliath's ancestors could have motivated David to build a provocative monument at the place of Goliath's skull just as much as Bible Hill's strategic

9. See 1 Sam 26:13–15.

10. See Hoffmeier, "David's Triumph," 108.

11. See Birch, "Golgotha on Mount Zion," 147.

12. See Garsiel, "David's Warfare," 160–64.

13. See Donnelly and Morrison, "Gigantism," 86.

location facing toward Philistine territory. Also, according to the book of First Chronicles, David set up a strategic monument on his eastern border facing his enemies across the Euphrates River.[14] This proves David could have done the same thing on the Shoulder of Hinnom. Finally, according to Dr. Gabriel Barkay, there are twenty funerary monuments located five miles west of Bible Hill that probably originated with King David.[15] If this is correct, it means David likely commissioned the construction of at least one of the funerary monuments near the Shoulder of Hinnom, which bolsters the contention that he would have built a similar monument at Bible Hill. (As a side note, excavations indicate the first-century quarry on the northeastern slope of Bible Hill would have likely destroyed any remnants of a Davidic monument there from the tenth century BCE.[16] This could explain why no trace of an actual monument commemorating the place of Goliath's skull has ever been found on Bible Hill.)

14. See 1 Chr 18:3.

15. Barkay, "Mounds," 32–39.

16. See Barkay et al., "Iron Age Fortress," 67.

8

What About the Skull of Adam?

NO MATTER HOW IMPROBABLE the legend of Adam's skull at Calvary may sound to modern ears, "there can be no doubt with regard to its general acceptance, in its simplest form, by [many of the Church Fathers]."[1] It would be shortsighted therefore to ignore this legend and its possible connection to Bible Hill as Golgotha. According to tradition, it was Noah's son Shem who originally buried Adam's skull somewhere around Jerusalem. Then, two generations later, Melchizedek (who was the king and high priest of Jerusalem) guarded it in the time of Abraham. Tradition does not specify exactly where Shem buried Adam's skull. If he buried it in the Valley of Shaveh where Abraham met Melchizedek, however, the skull of the first man could be at Bible Hill. Consider the following evidence.

In the tenth century BCE, King David's son Absalom erected a marble pillar a quarter mile from Jerusalem in the Valley of Shaveh where Abraham met Melchizedek.[2] It so happens the distance between Mount Zion and Bible Hill is a quarter mile. Plus, according to Josephus, Mount Zion was part of Jerusalem as early

1. C. Wilson, *Holy Sepulchre*, 6.

2. See Josephus, *Antiquities* 7.243; and McClintock and Strong, "Shaveh," para. 1.

as Joshua's conquest of Canaan in the thirteenth century BCE, which indicates it was part of the city when Absalom erected his marble pillar in the tenth century BCE.[3] Bible Hill also sits in a broad valley like the Valley of Shaveh. All this demonstrates that Absalom could have erected his marble pillar by Bible Hill. That, in turn, shows that Abraham could have met Melchizedek on the Shoulder of Hinnom as well. Moreover, as reported by the Russian Abbot Daniel (on pilgrimage 1106–7 CE), Abraham left his donkeys just south of Bible Hill before taking his son Isaac to Mount Moriah.[4] If this is accurate, it locates Abraham in the vicinity of the Shoulder of Hinnom following his encounter with Melchizedek. This further boosts the plausibility that somewhere near Bible Hill is the place where Abraham met Melchizedek. In that context, if Shem buried Adam's skull where Abraham met Melchizedek, then the skull of Adam could be at Bible Hill.

Astonishingly, one Eastern tradition lends credence to the above scenario. According to this tradition, Adam's skull was buried under the present-day Monastery of the Cross, just one mile west of Bible Hill.[5] The fact that a tradition exists linking the skull of Adam with a site so near Bible Hill (instead of the traditional Calvary) is not only shocking but also raises the chances that Bible Hill is Golgotha. It is also notable that, according to Scripture, the Valley of Shaveh (where Abraham met Melchizedek) was also called the "King's Valley."[6] This means, if Abraham met Melchizedek on the Shoulder of Hinnom, and if Bible Hill is Golgotha, then Jesus was crucified in the "Valley of the King." This is noteworthy because two of the titles for Jesus are the "King of the Jews" and the "King of kings."[7]

While evidence suggests Abraham met Melchizedek on the Shoulder of Hinnom, the odds still favor the skull of Calvary being

3. Josephus, *Antiquities* 7.65–68.

4. Daniel, *Pilgrimage of the Russian Abbot*, 38.

5. Guerin, *Géographique*, 79–80.

6. See Gen 14:17.

7. See the map of the King's Valley in Lipschits et al., *Ramat Rahel IV*, 9. See also Rev 17:14.

Goliath's. To be certain, in the words of Saint Jerome (writing in 398 CE), "Outside the city and outside the gate there are places where the heads of the condemned are cut off. This is where [the Gospels] took the name 'of the Skull' (*Calvariae*) . . . . It appears [accordingly that] Calvary signifies not the tomb of the first man [Adam], but the 'place of the decapitated.'"[8] What's more, a Byzantine lectionary (ca. 650 CE) corroborates Jerome's testimony when it mentions a place called "Golgotha" in the vicinity of Bethlehem.[9] Additionally, Jerome elsewhere calls the Adam legend a "stage miracle."[10] Therefore, logic suggests the proto-skull of Calvary would belong to someone decapitated like Goliath.

As a side note, perhaps the origin of these various Calvaries in the time of Jerome lies with Roman soldiers.[11] Following the conquest of Jerusalem by Rome in 70 CE, troops of the X Roman Legion were stationed on Mount Zion for 230 years. In that light, perhaps, over the centuries, successive cohorts of legionnaires assigned to Jerusalem assimilated and incorporated various local words and customs into the X Legion's subculture. If so, it would make sense that the legionnaires in Jerusalem could have started calling every place they decapitated prisoners in the Holy City "Golgotha" on the basis of a shallow understanding of the word and its related traditions. If this is accurate, it would help explain how the historical Golgotha got lost in the shuffle before Queen Helena and Bishop Macarius started looking for it. It could also explain why St. Willibald accusingly stated that Calvary was outside Jerusalem until Helena moved it inside the city.[12]

8. Jerome, *Commentary on Matthew*, 315–16.

9. See Saller and Bagatti, *Town of Nebo*, 196–97. It was not a place of beheading in the seventh century, however.

10. See C. Wilson, *Holy Sepulchre*, 163.

11. See Weksler-Bdolah, *Aelia Capitolina*, 19–50.

12. See Willibald, *Hodoeporicon*, 19.

A Monument at Bible Hill Reminiscent of Absalom's Pillar[13]

13. "Swords into Plowshares," photo by David Shay, Aug. 2008. Wikimedia Commons, CCBY-SA 3.0. https://commons.wikimedia.org/wiki/File:Swords_into_Plowshares.JPG.

9

The Monument of the Skull

If Bible Hill is the site where Jesus was crucified, buried, and reportedly resurrected from the dead, why would all the Evangelists refer to such a significant landmark merely as a "place"? Likewise, why would King David refer to a regal monument over the skull of Goliath merely as the "Place" of the Skull? These questions, the critics would say, must be accounted for if Bible Hill is the actual Calvary of history. It so happens a plausible answer to these questions lies in one of the Hebrew words for place and its equivalent term in Aramaic.

The Hebrew word *yad* can mean "place," but it can also mean "monument," making *yad* a difficult word to translate. Take Deut 23:12 and 2 Sam 18:18 in the Bible for instance. In Deut 23:12, *yad* simply means a "place" where people go. In that light, when the Bible mentions Absalom's *yad* in 2 Sam 18:18, one might be tempted to translate *yad* again as "place" as did the King James Bible: "Now Absalom . . . reared up for himself a pillar . . . and it is called unto this day, Absalom's place." While the King James' translation of *yad* as "place" for 2 Sam 18:18 is technically correct, an even clearer translation would have been "monument." This is why the New King James Bible translates *yad* in 2 Sam 18:18 as follows: "Now Absalom . . . set up a pillar for himself . . . . And to this day it is called Absalom's Monument."

Like *yad* in Hebrew, the Aramaic word *aterah* can mean "place," but it can also mean "monument," making *aterah* a difficult word to translate. Take Deut 23:12 and 2 Sam 18:18 in the Targum Jonathan, for instance. In Deut 23:12, *aterah* simply means a "place" where people go. In view of this, when the Targum Jonathan mentions the *aterah*-of-Absalom in 2 Sam 18:18, one might be tempted to translate *aterah* again as "place" as in the "Place of Absalom." While this would be technically correct, an even clearer translation would be "monument." After all, just like Absalom's *yad*, the *aterah*-of-Absalom signifies the monumental pillar erected by Absalom, not a place.

Seeing as the "Place of Absalom" means the "Monument of Absalom" in both Hebrew and Aramaic, it follows that the "Place of the Skull" could also mean the "Monument of the Skull" in both Hebrew and Aramaic as well. What's more, as seen with Isa 56:5 in the Bible and the Targum Jonathan, both *yad* and *aterah* can stand alone and still mean "monument." In that light, if Bible Hill is Calvary where David buried Goliath's skull, then logic suggests the verses in Scripture relating to Golgotha could be translated as follows, explaining why David and the Evangelists called Bible Hill a "place":

1. They brought Jesus to the monument, Golgotha, which, being interpreted, means the Monument of the Skull (Mark 15:22).[1]
2. Having come to the monument called Golgotha, which is to say, the Monument of the Skull, they gave Jesus wine to drink (Matt 27:33–34).

1. The "place Golgotha" in Mark 15:22 could be a semitism rooted in David's original Hebrew name for Calvary, namely, the "Place Skull" (*Yad Gulgoleth*). To be sure, in Codex Bezae (ca. 400 CE), Calvary is literally called the "Place Golgotha" in Mark 15:22. Similarly, in Codex Sinaiticus (ca. 350 CE), Calvary is again called the "Place Golgotha" in Matt 27:33. In both instances, the Greek matches *Yad Gulgoleth* perfectly. It is also telling that the New American Bible, Jubilee Bible 2000, Svenska Bible 1917, Biblia de Jerusalem, and Atualizada Bible all translate "place Golgotha" in Mark 15:22 as "Place of Golgotha," which can mean "Monument of Golgotha" in Aramaic (i.e., *Aterah de Golgotha*). It is also notable that King David's monument on his eastern border is called "*yad*" in 1 Chr 18:3.

3. When they came to the monument called the Skull, there they crucified Jesus (Luke 23:33).
4. Bearing his own cross, Jesus went out to the [hill] called the Monument of the Skull, which is called Golgotha in Aramaic (John 19:17).

It is also critical to mention that, like the translation of 2 Sam 18:18 as the "Place of Absalom" in the King James Bible, the "Place of the Skull" would have been an accurate translation of the original Aramaic into the Greek of the Gospels. This deduction also holds true when comparing the monument in Isa 56:5 translated as "place" in the King James Bible, with the "place" called Golgotha in the Gospel narratives. So, this new interpretation of the word "place" as "monument" does nothing to diminish the veracity of Scripture. Plus, the cranial shape of Bible Hill would explain how, over the centuries, the Monument of the Skull could come to be identified with the entire hill and be called "Golgotha" for short. To be sure, even today, Bible Hill still looks like the top of Goliath's gigantic skull sticking up out of the ground.[2] On top of that, executing Jesus at a monument celebrating God's victory over Goliath would have been diabolical, explaining why Jesus in his mercy asked the Father to forgive those responsible for his execution as soon as he was nailed to the cross.

2. See Hertzberg, *I and II Samuel*, 153.

10

Outside the Walls

That Bible Hill was outside the walls of Jerusalem when Jesus was crucified is an indisputable fact.[1] This is salient because the Epistle to the Hebrews and the Gospel of John both make it clear that Jesus was crucified outside the walls of Jerusalem. At the same time, Bible Hill has been close to the walls of the Holy City since the reign of King Hezekiah (ca. 716–687 BCE), as excavations of the famous Broad Wall prove.[2] This is relevant to Bible Hill as Golgotha because the Gospel of John says Jesus was crucified near the city.[3] Even more convincing than the Broad Wall, however, is the fact that Bible Hill sits only a third of a mile away from Gabbatha (where Pontius Pilate sentenced Jesus to the cross), and a quarter of a mile away from Mount Zion (where the walls of Jerusalem stood in the time of Jesus).[4] What's more, since the Gospel of John also says the village of Bethany was near Jerusalem, it follows that Calvary could have theoretically been well over a mile away from the Holy City; Bethany was two miles from Jerusalem in the time of Jesus. This confirms that Bible Hill was unquestionably in close

1. See the maps in Gibson, "Trial of Jesus," 101; and H. Shanks, *Jerusalem*, 172.

2. See H. Shanks, *Jerusalem*, 80.

3. See John 19:20.

4. See the map in Gibson, "Trial of Jesus," 101.

proximity to the city according to Scripture, underpinning the contention that Bible Hill is Golgotha.

As a side note, evidence indicates the Epistle to the Hebrews was written around 64 CE to a house synagogue in Jerusalem before the outbreak of the First Jewish-Roman War (66–74 CE).[5] This is relevant to this chapter because Hebrews invites its first-century listeners to go forth to Jesus outside the walls of Jerusalem to suffer there as Jesus did.[6] This indicates that, when Hebrews was penned, the historical Calvary was probably still outside the walls of Jerusalem. Otherwise, the exhortation in Hebrews to go forth to Jesus outside the city to suffer there as Jesus did would make little sense. At the very least, it would lose much of its emotional impact. This inference does not favor the traditional Calvary, or Gordon's Calvary, because those sites were inside the walls of Jerusalem almost two decades before Hebrews was authored. It does favor Bible Hill as Golgotha, however, because Bible Hill was unquestionably outside the walls of Jerusalem no matter when exactly Hebrews was written.

5. See McClintock and Strong, "Hebrews," para. 38.

6. See Heb 13:13.

11

Demography of Jerusalem

In the opinion of the esteemed biblical scholar Dr. William S. McBirnie, "demographic factors [are] the most formidable reasons of all for doubting the validity of the location of the traditional or Latin Calvary."[1] In the time of Jesus, at least twenty thousand people lived inside the walls of Jerusalem while another five thousand to ten thousand lived outside the walls, mostly north and northwest of the Second Wall near the traditional Calvary.[2] Moreover, as reported by Josephus, the population of Jerusalem would always explode at Passover.[3] In that light, if Jesus was executed at the traditional Calvary, all the buildings, houses, and throngs of people in northwest Jerusalem would have likely blocked the view of the crucifixion from afar, thus violating Scripture.[4] To account for this, the distinguished professor Dr. Joachim Jeremias suggests the disciples watched the execution while standing on top of a city wall.[5] However, there is no indication in the literature that the people of Jerusalem were expected to climb the walls of the city to

1. McBirnie, *Authentic Tomb*, 64.

2. See Geva, "Jerusalem's Population," 144–48; Jeremias, *Jerusalem in the Time of Jesus*, 84; and H. Shanks, "Ancient Jerusalem," paras. 1–6.

3. Josephus, *War* 2.280, 6.423–425.

4. See McBirnie, *Authentic Tomb*, 64, 73.

5. Jeremias, *Golgotha*, 3.

view executions.[6] Besides, even if people could stand on the walls to watch executions, the chances are still remote that Pilate would have crucified Jesus at an unfortified position near the bustling neighborhoods of Bezetha.[7] After all, according to Scripture, Jesus was still highly popular in Jerusalem on the day of his execution.[8] This means, if Pilate crucified Jesus at the traditional Calvary, it could have triggered a massive riot in Bezetha involving thousands of people attacking his troops. A riot of this sort during Passover was the last thing Pilate wanted.[9] Furthermore, to protect themselves from violent attacks, it is also unlikely that Pilate's troops would have rushed Jesus away to the traditional Calvary just to crucify him there at the first convenient spot.[10]

Viewing Bible Hill from Afar[11]

6. Gibson and Taylor, *Beneath the Church*, 59.

7. See J. Chadwick, "Revisiting Golgotha," 18–20. *Bezetha* was the name of the populated area to the north and northwest of the Second Wall at the time of Jesus.

8. See Luke 23:26–31.

9. See Matt 27:24.

10. See Tenz, "Golgotha or Calvary," 248.

11. "Buildings and Vegetation Around Jerusalem," photo by Willem van de Poll, 1964. Copyright Dutch National Archives, CC0.

12

The Praetorium

One of the keys to identifying the historical Golgotha is knowing the location, layout, and functions of the Praetorium where Jesus was condemned to the cross by Pontius Pilate. For this reason, this chapter presents a condensed description of the Praetorium. This will, in turn, serve as a foundation for subsequent chapters, and ultimately serve as evidence supporting the assertion that Bible Hill is the historical Golgotha.

The royal palace of King Herod was built on Jerusalem's western hill in the last quarter of the first century BCE. It was the second most important building in Jerusalem at the time of Jesus. Only the Temple exceeded it in significance. According to the distinguished biblical scholar Prof. Gustaf Dalman, while Herod the Great reigned in Judea, the local name for his palace in Jerusalem was "Camp of the King."[1] Once Roman governors moved in, however, the name apparently changed to Bethso, which means "House of the Commander" in Aramaic—a direct translation of the Latin word *praetorium.*[2]

1. Dalman, *Sacred Sites*, 274–75.

2. See Beswick, "Place Called Bethso," 108–9; and McClintock and Strong, "Praetorium," para. 1. Also note that Josephus never uses the term "Praetorium" anywhere in his writings, bolstering the plausibility that *Bethso* was his go-to word for the Praetorium. In addition, Philo of Alexandria similarly calls

The Praetorium was divided into five sectors, running north to south. The service buildings, kitchens, and storerooms were in the northernmost sector, around today's Tower of David Museum. This area was surrounded to the northwest by the fortifications of the city and by several colossal towers.[3] Below the service area lay the residential sector. This is where Roman governors such as Pontius Pilate most likely lived. This sector contained twin wings (the Caesareum and Agrippium), both of which were elevated on an enormous podium, parts of which have been excavated in archaeological digs. Below the residential area was a stunning pleasure garden with beautiful trees and fabulous ponds studded with bronze figurines and elegant dovecotes. Beyond the gardens lay the tribunal complex of the Praetorium, which included an imposing open-air platform facing Bible Hill called Gabbatha where crowds could gather outside the palace to participate in judicial proceedings.[4] The inside of the tribunal complex was equipped with holding cells and a courtyard for scourging prisoners.[5] The last and southernmost sector of the Praetorium was a fortified military camp.[6] According to the eminent archaeologist Dr. Carl Kraeling, a garrison of at least five hundred soldiers lived in this

Herod's palace the "House of the Procurators," which signifies the house of the Roman commanders in Jerusalem. For full disclosure, however, here is a list of the most popular translations of Bethso: According to Beswick, *Bethso* could mean "House of the Commander" (*beth tzoh*) or "House of Interdiction" (*beth tzo*) ("Place Called Bethso"). Caspari says *Bethso* means "House of Destruction" (*beth sho*), which symbolizes Gehenna (*Life of Christ*, 260). Chaplin says *Bethso* means "House of the Scarp" (*beth sur*), which corresponds to the "Rock Scarp of Zion" (see Conder, "Survey of Palestine," 169). Pixner says *Bethso* means "House of Dung" (*beth zoah*), which refers to Essene latrines on Mount Zion ("Essene Gateway," para. 37).

3. Gibson, "Trial of Jesus," 110.

4. Josephus reinforces this representation by describing Gabbatha as the "tribunal" of King Herod's royal palace on Mount Zion where Roman governors such as Pontius Pilate and Gessius Florus would set up their "judgment seats" before crowds of people in front of the palace. Compare Josephus, *War* 2.175–176, 2.301; Matt 27:19; and John 19:13. See also Kreyenbuhl, "Verurteilung Jesu," 15–22.

5. See Mark 15:16.

6. Dalman, *Sacred Sites*, 275, 336–37.

military camp, and its existence is documented by Josephus.[7] Evidence also suggests that within the military camp there would have been an armory, mess halls, infirmary, barracks, jail, latrines, and force-protection infrastructure.[8] In addition, a large fortified gate on the camp's western perimeter has been excavated.[9] This gate was highly strategic, allowing armed platoons to deploy rapidly out of the military camp. Logic suggests top officials in Jerusalem such as the high priest Caiaphas would have been permitted to enter and exit the city through this gate as well.

As a side note, according to the Bible, Peter was arrested and imprisoned (apparently in Jerusalem) by King Herod Agrippa during Passover. Before Agrippa could execute him, however, Peter escaped from prison and fled the city. If Peter escaped from the Praetorium's military camp as Scripture suggests, it would be logical to assume that, upon finding himself free, Peter immediately walked to John Mark's house and then slipped out of Jerusalem through the Essene Gate.[10] The Essene Gate was located on the southwestern lip of Mount Zion, facing directly toward Bible Hill.[11] It was named for the enigmatic sect of Jews called the Essenes whose priests rejected the Temple establishment in Jerusalem, preferring to worship God on their own terms.[12] In the time of Jesus, as one would expect, the Essenes of Jerusalem seem to have lived in a neighborhood by the Essene Gate.[13] Peter would have likely known these Essenes because of his connection with John the Baptist, who, according to tradition, grew up near Mount Zion and who was likely an Essene himself.[14]

7. Kraeling, "Roman Standards," 269. See also Josephus, *War* 2.328–329.

8. See Bishop, *Legionary Fortresses*, 17–38.

9. Gibson, "Bethso," 29.

10. See Gibson, "Trial of Jesus," 117. Also, it was Theodosius who first recorded (ca. 530 CE) that John Mark's house was on Mount Zion in the Apostolic Age; see Watson, "Sites of Sion," 205.

11. See Pixner, *Messiah*, 422.

12. See Riesner, "Primitive Community," 208–10.

13. See Ben-Daniel, *Mount Arbel*, 37–72.

14. See Betz, "John the Baptist," 18–25; John 1:40; and Schick, "Birthplace,"

The Ruins of Gabbatha[15]

62.

15. "Walls of the Old City of Jerusalem as the Sun Sets," photo by Wilson44691, May 22, 2009. Wikimedia Commons, CC0 1.0 Universal Deed. https://commons.wikimedia.org/wiki/File:Jerusalem_Walls_Golden.JPG.

13

The Rival Praetoriums

To RATIONALIZE JESUS' CRUCIFIXION at the traditional Calvary, some scholars maintain that the Praetorium must have been located in the Antonia Fortress or in the Hasmonean Palace.[1] However, according to Dr. Shimon Gibson, "it is unlikely Jesus was tried at the Antonia since it served primarily as a military observation tower with a very specific function: to keep an eye on the activities of the Jewish worshippers on the Temple Mount and to prevent rioting or demonstrations there."[2] It is also noteworthy that the Antonia is always called "the barracks" in the only verses in Scripture that allude to it.[3] What's more, as stated by Philo of Alexandria (writing ca. 40 CE), it was at Herod's palace that Pontius Pilate dwelled in Jerusalem, not the Antonia Fortress or the Hasmonean Palace.[4] Additionally, the mock coronation of Jesus makes the most sense if it happened in the royal palace of Herod the Great. To be certain, consider this. According to the Synoptic Gospels, before he was crucified, Jesus was paraded around the courtyard of the Praetorium's tribunal complex wearing a kingly robe and a crown

1. See Pixner, *Messiah*, 266–90.
2. Gibson, *Final Days*, loc. 90.
3. See C. Wilson, *Holy Sepulchre*, 42.
4. See Gibson, *Final Days*, loc. 91.

of thorns while Pilate's soldiers sarcastically hailed him as "King of the Jews." This event almost certainly occurred in the royal palace of King Herod. No other site in Jerusalem would have highlighted so clearly the irony in this mock coronation of Jesus. Locating the Praetorium at King Herod's palace would also explain why Pilate (following the mock coronation) paraded Jesus around Gabbatha wearing a "crown of thorns" and a "kingly robe" as he derisively asked the Jews, "Shall I crucify your King?" Besides, as Major-General Charles Wilson notes, "[it] would have been derogatory to the dignity of an official of [Pilate's] rank to [have lived] in a building of less importance [than Herod's palace], and [Pilate's] neglect to occupy it would have been regarded [by the Jews] as a sign of weakness."[5]

5. C. Wilson, *Holy Sepulchre*, 41.

14

The Mansion of Caiaphas

One of the oldest traditions in Christianity is the tradition placing the mansion of the high priest Caiaphas on Mount Zion. It is impossible to know how far back this tradition goes, but the Bordeaux Pilgrim confirms it existed by 333 CE.[1] Plus, unlike Golgotha, this tradition has remained virtually uncontested to this day.[2]

The mansion of Caiaphas would have been more than the high priest's home. It would have served as his administrative headquarters in Jerusalem as well.[3] Caiaphas served as high priest for almost twenty years, which was longer than any other high priest of his era.[4] A tenure of this length in an age of ruthless political maneuvering reflects extreme efficiency and pragmatism on the part of Caiaphas.[5] Caiaphas had to communicate on a daily basis not only with the Roman commanders in the military camp but also with various other foreign dignitaries and a wide variety

1. See Watson, "Sites of Sion," 219.

2. See Murphy-O'Connor, *Holy Land*, loc. 119–21; and Watson, "Sites of Sion," 219.

3. See Bond, *Caiaphas*, 33–38.

4. See Crossan, *Who Killed Jesus?*, 148.

5. Bond, *Caiaphas*, 33–38.

of Jewish officials. He also had his priestly duties to manage. As a result, it makes sense that Caiaphas lived somewhere on Mount Zion with easy access to the Praetorium and near a direct route to the Temple. In addition, his mansion must have been equipped with administrative offices and a large council chamber to hold official meetings of the Sanhedrin (e.g., the morning trial of Jesus as recorded in the Gospel of Luke). To be certain, according to the Gospels of Matthew and John, the chief priests convened a "Sanhedrin" in the mansion of Caiaphas to plan the death of Jesus.[6] Moreover, other first-century mansions with offices and large meeting rooms have been excavated north of Mount Zion in the Herodian Quarter, boosting the odds that Caiaphas's mansion would have been designed similarly.[7] Scripture also supports the premise that the Sanhedrin met in Caiaphas's mansion (rather than the Chamber of Hewn Stone in the Temple) because, according to Acts 5:17–41, when the whole Sanhedrin convened, none of its members knew the apostles were in the Temple preaching. (The Sanhedrin had probably stopped convening in the Temple after Archelaus was deposed in 7 CE.)[8]

In view of the above, it is logical to assume that, following Jesus' arrest at Gethsemane and formal condemnation by the Sanhedrin the next morning in Caiaphas's mansion, the chief priests and elders would have delivered Jesus to Pilate's soldiers in a matter of minutes because the mansion of Caiaphas would have been close to the military camp of the Praetorium. Once Jesus was in Roman custody, Pilate's men would have led Jesus into the tribunal complex and locked him in a holding-cell while the members of the Sanhedrin walked around the Praetorium to Gabbatha. Meanwhile, some of the soldiers would have walked up to Pilate's residence in the Caesareum and informed the governor of the situation. On hearing the news, Pilate would have promptly put on his regalia and then walked down to the tribunal complex where he

6. See John 11:47 and Matt 26:3.

7. See Avigad, *Herodian Quarter*, 57.

8. See C. Wilson, *Holy Sepulchre*, 39–40.

would have seen Jesus in his holding-cell. At that point, the governor would have gone outside to Gabbatha through a fortified postern and then asked the chief priests and elders to explain to him why Jesus had been brought to the Praetorium.[9] After that, the events of the trial of Jesus would unfold, culminating in Jesus' crucifixion.

As a side note, there are currently three sites on Mount Zion that could be the location where the mansion of Caiaphas once stood. The one with the longest tradition of being the mansion of Caiaphas is St. Saviour Chapel, located just south of today's Armenian parking lot.[10] The second oldest site is the Church of St. Peter in Gallicantu, situated on the southeastern slope of Mount Zion with a breathtaking view of the Temple Mount and Mount Olivet. The third site is where the archaeologists of the Mount Zion Archaeological Project are presently excavating, about 135 yards east of the modern Zion Gate. All three sites are within earshot of one another and contain the ruins of ancient palatial mansions from the time of Jesus.

9. See John 18:29.

10. See Watson, "Sites of Sion," 199.

One of the Likely Sites for Caiaphas's Mansion on Mount Zion[11]

11. "Church on the Western Hill, 'Zion.' New Church of St. Peter. Called Galakanti or the Cock Crowing," photo by American Colony (Jerusalem), ca. 1931–34. Matson photograph collection, U.S. Library of Congress, used with permission.

15

Gethsemane

PERHAPS THE GARDEN OF Gethsemane (where Jesus was arrested) was somewhere in the "King's Garden" in the present Silwan area of East Jerusalem. To be sure, the King's Garden rests at the foot of the southernmost peak of Mount Olivet, and it sits in the Kidron Valley where the winter stream of Kidron would have been when Jesus was arrested.[1] Moreover, before the crucifixion, Jesus was establishing a new movement of baptism centered at the Pool of Siloam by the King's Garden, which means Jesus visited the King's Garden frequently in the months leading up to the passion.[2] This means the King's Garden meets the fundamental prerequisites needed to be the area surrounding Gethsemane in accordance with Scripture. Plus, the path from the traditional site of the Last Supper on Mount Zion (i.e., the Cenacle) down to the city gate facing the King's Garden would have been paved and illuminated at night in the first century.[3] In that light, it makes sense that Jesus

1. See Lee and Bain, *New Testament*, 103; and Souvay, "Mount Olivet," paras. 1–2.

2. See Gibson, *Final Days*, loc. 172.

3. The Cenacle refers to the house on Mount Zion where, according to ancient tradition, the apostles ate the Last Supper with Jesus, experienced the coming of the Holy Spirit at Pentecost, and resided when visiting Jerusalem during the Apostolic Age (see Clausen, *Upper Room*, loc. 140). For information

would have used this path to reach Gethsemane after celebrating the Passover meal with his disciples.[4] In addition, given the narrow window of time in which all of the events of the passion must have taken place, and considering that Jesus was already suffering from hematidrosis when he was arrested, it makes sense that Gethsemane would have been somewhere in the King's Garden near the traditional home of Caiaphas. What's more, if Jesus was arrested in the King's Garden, it would explain how he knew exactly when the arresting party would arrive to take him into custody: He would have seen the glow of the mob's torches descending down Mount Zion from his vantage point on one of the lower ridges of Mount Olivet. Scripture also suggests Caiaphas was given the authority to command a limited number of Roman troops stationed in Jerusalem.[5] If this is correct (and if Caiaphas's mansion was near the military camp of the Praetorium), it would explain how a detachment of legionnaires could come to Gethsemane (in the King's Garden) without Pilate knowing about it.[6] Additionally, since Jesus knew he would be arrested beforehand, the conspicuousness of the King's Garden would not have mattered to him. In fact, it would rationalize Jesus' indignant reaction to the overly armed arresting party at Gethsemane. It is also notable that, if Gethsemane was in the King's Garden (and if Caiaphas's mansion was on Mount Zion), it would explain how Peter could follow Jesus and the arresting party at a distance up to Caiaphas's mansion without getting lost or taken into custody in the process. Additionally, if the "King of Glory" was arrested in the "Garden of the King" as a common outlaw, the apostles would have surely seen the irony in this upon later reflection.[7] The evidence for Gethsemane being in the King's Garden is relevant to Bible Hill as Golgotha because it bolsters all the other evidence pointing toward the Shoulder of Hinnom as the historical site of Jesus' crucifixion.

---

on the path down Mount Zion, see Pixner, *Messiah*, 259.

4. See Luke 22:10–54.
5. See Matt 27:65.
6. See John 18:3.
7. See Mark 14:48 and Ps 24:7.

Viewing the Possible Site of Caiaphas's Mansion from Mount Olivet[8]

8. "'Mt. Zion' from Southern Slope of Olivet," photo by Matson Photo Service, Nov. 28, 1942. Matson photograph collection, U.S. Library of Congress, used with permission.

16

The Roman Rooster

PETER DENIED JESUS THREE times at Caiaphas's mansion before the rooster crowed twice (just as Jesus predicted would happen).[1] If Caiaphas's mansion was on Mount Zion, it stands to reason the second rooster crow was a Roman trumpet signaling the changing of the guard in the military camp of the Praetorium.[2] To be sure, consider that only a few days before Passover, Jesus mentioned this Roman "rooster crow" while preaching on Mount Olivet.[3] It follows then that the Roman "rooster crow" would have been fresh on Peter's mind when he denied Jesus.[4] As a result, if Peter heard the loud and unmistakable Roman "rooster crow" while standing in the courtyard of Caiaphas's mansion, logic suggests he would have immediately realized Jesus' prediction about his false bravery had come true. It would also explain how Jesus himself heard the second "rooster crow" so clearly despite being inside Caiaphas's judgment hall.[5] All this is relevant to Bible Hill as Golgotha because it reinforces all the other geographical evidence tying Jesus'

1. See Mark 14:30 and Matt 26:75.
2. See Humphries, *Mystery of the Last Supper*, 179.
3. See Mark 13:35.
4. See Humphries, *Mystery of the Last Supper*, 179.
5. See Luke 22:61.

passion to southwest Jerusalem. (As a side note, if the second rooster was a trumpet, then the first rooster must have been an actual cock riled up by all the ruckus near Caiaphas's mansion. This premise is bolstered by the fact that Jesus loved using puns, as Peter would have known all too well.)[6]

6. See Stein, *Jesus' Teachings*, 12–14.

17

The Tower of Mariamne

As Pilate stood atop Gabbatha debating the crowd about the fate of Jesus, the chief priests revealed that Jesus was Galilean.[1] This meant Jesus was subject to the authority of Herod Antipas, the governor of Galilee.[2] So, Pilate ordered his troops to escort Jesus to Herod Antipas for judgment, as Antipas was in Jerusalem for Passover. The Gospel of Luke does not specify where Jesus met Antipas, but the Gospel of John and the Gospel of Mark provide two vital clues: It was somewhere the chief priests could not conceivably become ritually impure, and it had to be somewhere close to Gabbatha to rationalize Jesus being crucified as early as the "third hour" (9:00 a.m.).[3] This indicates Antipas was in the Tower of Mariamne.

Located roughly a hundred yards north of Gabbatha, the Tower of Mariamne was a major component of the fortifications of the Praetorium along its western wall.[4] Josephus says of this tower: "Named after Queen Mariamne, [it] was solid to a height of twenty feet, being equally twenty feet in breadth and length. Its

1. See Luke 23:6.
2. See Luke 23:7.
3. See John 18:28.
4. See Gibson, "Trial of Jesus," 110.

upper living quarters were finer and more varied than the other towers [of the palace], for [Herod] thought it best to adorn the [tower] named after his wife more than those named after men .... [Its] entire height was fifty feet. Such were the dimensions but due to [its] location [it] appeared much taller."[5]

If Antipas was in the Tower of Mariamne, then Scripture dictates that Pilate quickly and securely sent Jesus up there to see him. At the same time, the chief priests would have quickly walked up the road to the Tower of Mariamne where they could yell at Antipas from below, avoiding ritual defilement. Once Antipas finished mocking Jesus with his "splendid apparel," Scripture says he ordered the would-be Messiah returned to Pilate (apparently still wearing his splendid apparel). At that point the chief priests would have hustled back to Gabbatha to stir up the crowd against Jesus before his trial recommenced. As soon as Jesus returned to his holding-cell, Pilate's men must have removed his splendid apparel. This would account for the purple robe that Pilate's troops would later use in Jesus' mock coronation in the palace courtyard.[6]

The major link between Antipas and the Tower of Mariamne, however, is Bible Hill. The Gospel of Luke bluntly states that Antipas had been plotting to kill Jesus well before the two men met face to face in Jerusalem. To be certain, as Jesus approached the Holy City for Passover, people were already warning him to stay

5. Josephus, *War* 5.170–175. To avoid confusion, it should also be noted that the Tower of Mariamne is usually positioned on the northern end of the Praetorium in models and maps of first-century Jerusalem. According to the latest archaeological research, however, the Tower of Mariamne stood halfway along Jerusalem's present western city wall near the ruins of Gabbatha (see Gibson, "Trial of Jesus," 109). This research is reinforced by Josephus as well. In his description of the Roman siege of Jerusalem in 70 CE, the Jewish historian notes that, at the end of the conflict, General Titus ordered his troops to leave the Towers of Hippicus, Phasael, and Mariamne standing along with a portion of the western city wall that was attached to them (see C. Wilson, *Holy Sepulchre*, 142). This command by Titus makes the most sense if the Tower of Mariamne was located to the south of the other two towers because it would mean Titus was preserving a powerful defensive wall with massive watchtowers on each end to protect his troops that would be garrisoned on Mount Zion after he left Jerusalem (see Weksler-Bdolah, *Aelia Capitolina*, 24–26).

6. See Luke 23:11 and Mark 15:17.

away from Jerusalem because Herod Antipas wanted to kill him.[7] Antipas had Jesus in his crosshairs and longed to see him dead. Yet, unlike the other enemies of Jesus who came to Golgotha to watch Jesus get crucified, Antipas made no appearance at the crucifixion scene. This defies logic unless Antipas was in the Tower of Mariamne where he could watch the entire trial and execution of Jesus without going anywhere. There was precedence for such behavior as well. As noted by Josephus, the Hasmonean king Alexander Jannaeus (r. 103–76 BCE) watched eight hundred men get crucified in Jerusalem while he was drinking and cavorting with his concubines.[8] (As a side note, it is conceivable that Pilate's wife was in the Tower of Mariamne during the trial of Jesus as well. This would explain how she sent a message to Pilate just before he reached the point of no return regarding the fate of "that innocent man" called "Christ".)

The Likely Site of Mariamne's Tower by the Ruins of Gabbatha[9]

7. See Luke 13:31.

8. Josephus, *War* 1.97.

9. "West Side of the Old City (Jerusalem)," photo by Rhododendrites, Mar. 12, 2017. Wikimedia Commons, CCBY-SA 4.0. The image herein is a cropped version of the original. https://commons.wikimedia.org/wiki/File:West_side_of_the_Old_City_(20018).jpg.

18

Crown of Thorns

According to Israel's Ministry of Environmental Protection, Bible Hill is home to a wide variety of thorns. This is noteworthy because Pilate's soldiers used thorns to crown Jesus in the Praetorium.[1] "The likelihood is that lying around the soldiers' quarters [in the courtyard of the tribunal complex] . . . were quantities of thorn branches. With wood always being a scarce commodity around Jerusalem, the soldiers had probably gathered [piles of thorns there] as fuel for the fires to keep themselves warm during the cold Jerusalem nights."[2] Then, when Pilate ordered his men to scourge Jesus, "no doubt some bully . . . hit upon the idea of twisting some of the thorn branches into a mock crown, then performing a heavy-handed coronation upon [Jesus]."[3] Given the proximity of the military camp to the Shoulder of Hinnom, it follows that the branches used to weave Jesus' crown of thorns could have come from Bible Hill. This is noteworthy because it forensically correlates Bible Hill with a major event in Jesus' passion. It also correlates Pilate's soldiers with the Shoulder of Hinnom, thus boosting the probability that Bible Hill is Golgotha.

1. See Mark 15:17.
2. See I. Wilson, *Murder at Golgotha*, loc. 70.
3. I. Wilson, *Murder at Golgotha*, loc. 70.

19

The Scepter of Christ

In the time of Jesus, the wastewater of the Praetorium flowed through a monumental tunnel that extended under the Praetorium's western fortification wall.[1] When the Praetorium's wastewater flowed out of this sewer line, it would settle in a leach field just north of today's Hebron-Road Bridge.[2] In that light, it is possible a stand of giant reeds (*arundo donax*) was growing by this leach field in the time of Jesus, because the giant reed is an excellent plant for purifying wastewater.[3] Moreover, "[*arundo donax*] can adapt to various habitats and tolerate various adverse environmental conditions, such as cold temperatures, drought, flooding, and high salinity."[4] This means giant reeds could have survived in the Hinnom Valley with only the wastewater from the Praetorium to live on for long periods of time. What's more, the term "reed" appears frequently in the Bible, and some of these references almost certainly indicate *arundo donax*.[5] It makes sense, therefore, that giant reeds would have been planted around the Praetorium's leach

1. See Gibson, "Bethso," 26–27.

2. See Kloner, *Survey of Jerusalem*, 164–65; and Steel and McGhee, *Water Supply*, 576–77.

3. Zhang et al., "Giant Reed," 7.

4. Kato-Noguchi and Kato, "Invasive Mechanism," 4.

5. See Perdue, "Arundo donax," 368.

field to beautify this otherwise polluted area. Plus, "the stalks of the giant reed are hollow and hard like bamboo canes . . . and have been used to make fishing rods, [and] walking sticks."[6] It follows then that, if a stand of giant reeds grew in the Praetorium's leach field, one of Pilate's soldiers on his way to the military camp from the Shoulder of Hinnom could have cut one of the reeds down before he mocked and beat Jesus over the head with it later on in the Praetorium. Of course, this is speculative, but the reed used to bludgeon Jesus is not. It was real and most likely came from somewhere close to the military camp of the Praetorium such as the first-century leach field in the valley below Gabbatha. Perhaps Josephus even refers to this leach field when he mentions the "Serpents Pool" in his description of southwest Jerusalem. It makes sense, after all, that snakes would have been living in a dense stand of *arundo donax*, and the leach field may have looked like a swampy retaining pond during Jerusalem's rainy season. These conditions would have given rise to the name Serpents Pool.

6. MacKenzie, "Plants," 93.

20

The Judgment Gate

WHILE IT IS UNLIKELY that the verse in Hebrews saying Jesus suffered "outside the gate" refers to any specific gate in Jerusalem, nevertheless, Jesus did leave the Holy City through a specific gate to be crucified. What gate was it? Given what is known about Gabbatha from archaeological excavations on Mount Zion, the monumental gate excavated next to Gabbatha (where the military camp of the Praetorium was located in the time of Jesus) seems to be the most logical choice. This is bolstered by the ancient name for this gate, namely, the "Gate of Judgment"—through which Jesus left Jerusalem to be crucified at Calvary. In 1283, Buchard of Mount Zion had this to say about this gate: "The Judgment Gate is so called because the trial was heard before it and the condemned man passed through it on his way to [Golgotha]."[1]

Excavations of the Judgment Gate indicate its approach was originally thirty feet wide with paved steps leading up to the gate via a sloping embankment.[2] The gate itself was ten feet wide and would have been heavily guarded. As soldiers and civilians approached the Judgment Gate to enter the military camp of the Praetorium, they would have seen a fortified watchtower

1. Quoted in Keshman, "Footsteps," 90.

2. Gibson, "Bethso," 29.

on their right and the elevated platform of Gabbatha to their left. Excavations of the collapsed stone debris above the approach to the gateway suggest the outer infrastructure of the Judgment Gate was destroyed during the Roman siege of Jerusalem in 70 CE. The gate itself remained intact, however, and maintained its utility for another fifteen hundred years—though on a much smaller scale. In the year 985, for instance, the Gate of Judgment makes a brief cameo when the Arab geographer al-Muqaddas lists the "Tribunal-Palace Gate" among the gates of Jerusalem.[3] Then, in 1495, the Muslim historian Mujir al-Din mentions the Judgment Gate as the "Secret Gate" between the Jaffa Gate and Zion Gate near the old Armenian gardens.[4]

As a side note, according to some experts, the Epistle to the Hebrews was not only written to a house synagogue in Jerusalem, but was specially addressed to Essene priests living on Mount Zion who had accepted Jesus as the Messiah.[5] If this is accurate (and if Bible Hill is Golgotha), then, from the subjective point of view of the Essenes listening to Hebrews, the gate facing Calvary (mentioned in v. 13:12) would have been referring to their own gate, the Essene Gate, from which many of them would have witnessed the crucifixion of Jesus on the Shoulder of Hinnom firsthand. This boosts the chances of Bible Hill being Golgotha because it further undercuts the idea that "the gate" facing Calvary in Heb 13:12 must be an allusion to the main eastern gate of the Temple, as advocated by supporters of the miphkad altar theory of Calvary.

3. See Le Strange, *Palestine*, 212–17; and C. Wilson, *Holy Sepulchre*, 145.

4. See Le Strange, *Palestine*, 212–17.

5. See McClintock and Strong, "Hebrews," para. 38; Parsons, "Son and High Priest," 197; Pixner, *Messiah*, 366–67; and Yadin, "Melchizedek and Qumran," 152–54.

Viewing Bible Hill from the Ruins of the Judgment Gate[6]

6. "People Crossing the Valley of Hinnom Near the Sultan's Pool," June–Aug. 1950. The Meitar Collection and the Pritzker Family National Collection of Photographs, The National Library of Israel. Public domain.

21

Prisoner Transport

If Bible Hill is Calvary, Pilate would have never sent Jesus there with only four guards by his side. Dozens more security experts would have been working diligently to safeguard the entire trek from the Judgment Gate to Golgotha.[1] This is not baseless speculation either. According to Josephus, Pilate used undercover operatives to gather intelligence in Jerusalem.[2] Surely he would have used his covert operatives to assess risks pertinent to prisoner transport as well. Josephus also implies that Pilate vetted and disarmed everyone approaching Gabbatha when he conducted business there.[3] It stands to reason then that Pilate vetted and disarmed everyone approaching Gabbatha when he put the highly popular prisoner called "Christ" on trial, ensuring the safety of his soldiers should "Christ" be sentenced to death. (According to the British historian Ian Wilson, almost everyone in the crowd at Gabbatha wanted Jesus to be crucified despite his popularity because the crowd consisted mainly of vetted allies of Caiaphas.)[4] It also appears a sally port existed in the time of Jesus at today's Jerusalem

1. See Gibson, *Final Days*, loc. 105.
2. Josephus, *Antiquities* 18.60–62.
3. See Josephus, *War* 2.175–177.
4. I. Wilson, *Murder at Golgotha*, loc. 76.

University College.[5] If this is accurate, it means cavalrymen could have quickly burst forth to attack any runaway prisoners or rioters on the main road to Calvary during prisoner transport. Finally, if unforeseen disturbances still arose despite all these security measures, rapid communication between the Praetorium, sally port, and Bible Hill via trumpet blasts and flag signaling would have enabled Pilate's men to coordinate their efforts to eliminate the threat.[6]

5. See Conder, "Rock Scarp," 84. However, in the opinion of Fr. Bargil Pixner, there was no sally port at this site, but rather an Essene latrine (see Pixner, *Messiah*, 201).

6. See Josephus, *War* 2.579; and Woolliscroft, *Military Signaling*, 21.

22

The Stone Bridge to Calvary

EVIDENCE SUGGESTS, IN THE time of Jesus, a stone bridge crossed the Hinnom Valley where the Hebron-Road Bridge is located today. To be sure, according to Adamnan (writing in 670 CE), the stone bridge that connected Mount Zion to the Shoulder of Hinnom in his day was the very bridge from which Judas Iscariot hanged himself after Jesus had been condemned to the cross.[1] What's more, given that several first-century stone bridges are still in existence even now, it is certainly possible that the bridge cited by Adamnan did exist when Jesus was crucified.[2] If this was the case (and if Bible Hill is Calvary), it would explain how the chief priests traveled from the Praetorium to Golgotha without becoming ritually defiled by the various sources of impurity in the valley below. It is also notable that (assuming Bible Hill is Calvary), if a stone bridge connected the Praetorium to the Shoulder of Hinnom in the time of Jesus, Pilate could have easily ridden out to Calvary to put a new *titulus* on the cross of Jesus himself. This would rationalize the scene in the Gospel of John where the chief priests are forcefully opposing Pilate for doing this after Jesus had already been nailed to the cross. It would also help explain why

1. Adamnan, *Arculfus*, 19.
2. See O'Connor, *Roman Bridges*, 188.

the wording on the *titulus* varies depending on which Gospel one reads. Finally, a stone bridge connecting Mount Zion with the Shoulder of Hinnom would have accommodated horses, camels, and the throngs of pilgrims entering Jerusalem from the southwest during the Jewish festivals, boosting the odds that such a bridge existed there in the first century. This, in turn, further underpins the premise that Bible Hill is Calvary.

The Suggested Site of the Stone Bridge to Calvary[3]

3. "Lower Pool of Gihon," photographer unknown, ca. 1898–1946. Matson photograph collection, U.S. Library of Congress, used with permission.

23

Physical Injury

WHEN JESUS LEFT JERUSALEM through the Judgment Gate, he was already suffering from the debilitating effects of severe blood loss and dehydration.[1] To be blunt, in Jesus' brutalized condition, there was no way he could have crossed the Hinnom Valley and marched up to Bible Hill with a *patibulum* on his shoulders.[2] As a result (if Bible Hill is Golgotha), it makes sense that Pilate's troops would have seized Simon of Cyrene on the eastern side of the stone bridge to Calvary, and forced him to carry Jesus' *patibulum* up the Shoulder of Hinnom to Bible Hill. Indeed, as the distinguished professor Lucien Gautier explains, "The fact that . . . the soldiers want [Simon of Cyrene] to carry the cross [shows] that the place of the crucifixion was not in the immediate proximity [of Gabbatha]."[3] What's more, seizing Simon of Cyrene on the eastern side of the stone bridge to Calvary comports with archaeology. This is because, in the time of Jesus, the eastern side of this bridge would have been right below the sally port described in chapter 21 on prisoner transport. This sally port would have provided vital cover for the guards as they secured Jesus' *patibulum* onto Simon

1. Edwards et al., "Physical Death," 1455–63.
2. See I. Wilson, *Murder at Golgotha*, loc. 82.
3. Gautier, "Remarks," 78.

of Cyrene's back. It is also logical to assume that, as the *patibulum* was being transferred to Simon, Jesus talked to the women of Jerusalem.[4] Naturally, all this boosts the odds of Bible Hill being Golgotha because the evidence once again harmonizes perfectly with Scripture and archaeology.

The Ascent to Bible Hill[5]

4. See Luke 23:26–31.

5. "State Visit to Jerusalem of Wilhelm II of Germany in 1898. Emperor Riding with Group; the Citadel, and West City Wall Are in Background," photo by American Colony (Jerusalem), ca. Oct. 26–Nov. 4, 1898. Matson photograph collection, U.S. Library of Congress, used with permission.

24

The Road of the Patriarchs

Bible Hill overlooks a major road in southwest Jerusalem called the Road of the Patriarchs where thousands of pilgrims were streaming into the city on the day Jesus was crucified.[1] The Road of the Patriarchs is the ancient north-south route crossing the land of Israel where, according to Dr. Rivkah Adler, "80% of the events of the Bible happened."[2] The Road of the Patriarchs starts in Megiddo in the north and passes through Shechem, Bethel, Jerusalem, Bethlehem, and Hebron until it ends in Beersheba in the south. This road has always been a significant international thoroughfare as well, as the ancient coins from Greece, Assyria, Nabataea, and Ethiopia excavated on the Shoulder of Hinnom confirm.[3] Moreover, as John Poloner (on pilgrimage in 1421 CE) explains, "many mystical events have come to pass [on the Road of the Patriarchs]. Abraham and his wife passed along this road when they came from Chaldaea . . . . The patriarch Jacob and his wife Rachel often passed over it. The Blessed Virgin Mary when pregnant went . . . along this road and rested when weary . . . . Also Isaiah and Elijah and many of the holy prophets when going to the Holy City, passed along this road."[4] Additionally, the stretch of

1. See Schiffer, "Take a Journey," para. 1.

2. Adler, "Way of the Patriarchs," para. 1.

3. See Barkay, "Slope of the Hinnom Valley," 99, 106; and Barkay, *Ketef Hinnom*, 13, 18, 29.

4. Poloner, *Description of the Holy Land*, 20.

the Road of the Patriarchs between Jerusalem and Bethlehem has been known as the "royal road" since at least the seventh century.[5] If this tradition extends back to the first century (and if Bible Hill is Golgotha), then the "King of the Jews" walked up the "Road of Royalty" to be crucified at Calvary. What's more, since most of the events recorded in the Hebrew Bible occurred in the vicinity of the Road of the Patriarchs, it stands to reason the crucifixion of Jesus probably took place along this road as well.

As a side note, the ruins of another ancient road were excavated on Bible Hill in the 1970s.[6] This road curved around the northern slope of Bible Hill until it intersected with the Road of the Patriarchs.[7] The age of this road is unknown as indicated by the contradictory dates assigned to it in the literature.[8] If this road existed in the first century, however, it may be assumed Jesus was walking on it when his executioners offered him wine to drink just before they crucified him.[9]

The Road of the Patriarchs[10]

5. See Adamnan, *Arculfus*, 31; and Fabri, *Wanderings*, 541.

6. Barkay, "Slope of the Hinnom Valley," 100.

7. See Thompson, "Oldest Biblical Text," para. 5.

8. See Barkay, "Slope of the Hinnom Valley," 100; Perrot et al., "Notes and News," 58; and Zionsberg Jerusalem, "Gates," para. 1.

9. See Mark 15:23.

10. "Jerusalem (El-Kouds). First View of Jerusalem from the South," photo by American Colony (Jerusalem), ca. 1898–1907. Matson photograph collection, U.S. Library of Congress, used with permission.

25

Mulberry Vinegar

JESUS TOLD HIS DISCIPLES at the Last Supper that he would never drink the fruit of the vine again while he was alive.[1] So, when the soldiers offered Jesus wine to drink at Golgotha, he immediately rejected it. Yet the Gospel of John has Jesus drinking sour wine on the cross.[2] This seems contradictory. There is a rational explanation, however, if Jesus was crucified on Bible Hill. Roman soldiers frequently drank cheap sour wine called *posca*.[3] While *posca* was universally drunk by soldiers across the empire, the recipe for this drink was anything but universal. As a result, Roman soldiers would take what they could find locally and make *posca* with it. This is why the soldiers at Bible Hill may have made *posca* from mulberries. The land surrounding Bible Hill has been historically covered with mulberry trees.[4] Mulberries also make excellent sour wine, and they grow on trees, not vines. So, if Jesus drank mulberry vinegar on the cross, it means he was not drinking the fruit of the vine, but rather, the fruit of the tree. Moreover, Jesus was familiar with mulberries, so it stands to reason he would have known the

1. See Matt 26:29.
2. See John 19:28.
3. See Roth, *Logistics*, 37; and Manning, *Holy Fields*, 105.
4. See Barkay, "Riches of Ketef Hinnom," 25.

difference between real wine and mulberry vinegar.[5] It may be assumed therefore that Jesus probably saw a jar of mulberry *posca* while hanging on the cross and knew it was acceptable for him to drink. This inference undergirds the premise that Bible Hill is Calvary because it explains how Jesus fulfilled Psalm 69:21 on the cross without drinking the fruit of the vine.

5. See Luke 17:6.

26

Casting Lots

ACCORDING TO SCRIPTURE, THE soldiers who crucified Jesus cast lots to see which one of them would get Jesus' seamless tunic.[1] While no evidence of gambling from the first century has been excavated on Bible Hill, nevertheless, the playing-dice of Ottoman soldiers stationed there have been found.[2] This proves soldiers have gambled on Bible Hill in the past, reinforcing the prospect that Roman soldiers would have cast lots on Bible Hill in the time of Jesus.

As a side note, in the opinion of some scholars, the seamless tunic Jesus wore at Calvary symbolizes the high priesthood of Christ.[3] If this is correct and if Bible Hill is Calvary, where also Abraham met Melchizedek, it means Jesus walked to Golgotha wearing a royal crown and a priestly vestment in the likeness of Melchizedek, who was both king and high priest of Jerusalem when he walked to the Shoulder of Hinnom to greet Abraham. This uncanny similarity between Jesus and Melchizedek would have surely been apparent to the apostles upon later reflection, explaining why Jesus is compared to Melchizedek so often in the Epistle to the Hebrews.

1. See John 19:23–24.
2. See Barkay, *Ketef Hinnom*, 12.
3. See Lane, "Jesus as High Priest," para. 2

27

The True Cross

Excavations on the Shoulder of Hinnom confirm that, during the Ottoman period, Turkish soldiers stored weapons and other gear in one of the burial caves on the northern slope of Bible Hill.[1] This means the Roman soldiers could have done the same in the time of Jesus. If they did, it would certainly explain how the soldiers who executed Jesus would have conveniently accessed spears, nails, ropes, stipes, wine, vinegar, gall, myrrh, and other such supplies at Golgotha. This possibility is not built on pure speculation either. It is buttressed by the excavations on the northern slope of Bible Hill that uncovered two axes, an iron wedge, and a plethora of pottery fragments from the late Second Temple period, along with coins of the Roman procurators Coponius, Valerius-Gratus, and Pontius Pilate.[2] Therefore, it is likely that, following Jesus' crucifixion, the historical stipe of the true cross would have been duly stored in one of the burial caves at Bible Hill to be used again. Indeed, as Joseph Zias and Eliezer Sekeles note, "One can reasonably assume that the scarcity of wood [in Jerusalem] may have been expressed in the economics of crucifixion in that the cross bar, as well as the

1. See Barkay, *Ketef Hinnom*, 12.
2. Barkay, *Ketef Hinnom*, 18; and Barkay, "Riches of Ketef Hinnom," 28.

upright, would [have been] used repeatedly."[3] Storing all the stipes discreetly in a cave would have also accommodated Jewish sentiment against displaying instruments of execution publicly.

Tradition also says the wood for the true cross came from a site only one mile west of Bible Hill at the Monastery of the Cross in the Valley of the Cross.[4] If this is true, it certainly sustains the premise that Bible Hill is Golgotha from a logistical perspective. It is also worth mentioning that, according to one Jewish tradition, the Monastery of the Cross was also the Place of Stoning.[5] If this is accurate (and if Bible Hill is the Place of Beheading), it means, in the time of Jesus, the two main execution sites in Jerusalem were only one mile apart, creating an "execution corridor" in southwest Jerusalem. In this light, it is conceivable that the apostle Paul, at the behest of Caiaphas, followed Saint Stephen through the Judgment Gate, up the Shoulder of Hinnom, past Bible Hill, to the Place of Stoning in the Valley of the Cross where he watched the first Christian martyr get executed.[6] This possibility is buttressed by three medieval pilgrims—Eugesippus (on pilgrimage in 1140 CE), John of Wurzburg (on pilgrimage in 1160 CE), and Fetellus (on pilgrimage in 1175 CE)—who all say Saint Stephen was stoned somewhere west of Jerusalem.[7] Moreover, according to the Babylonian Talmud, Jesus was both stoned and crucified at Calvary, a tradition that correlates the Place of Stoning with Golgotha.[8] This correlation would actually make sense if the Place of Stoning had been relatively close to Calvary in the time of Jesus, causing later generations to inadvertently conflate memories related to these two places (such as the crucifixion of Jesus and the stoning of Saint Stephen).

3. Quoted in H. Shanks, "Scholar's Corner," para. 10.

4. See Saewulf, *Saewulf*, 20–21; and Tzapheres, "Monastery of the Cross," 32.

5. See Hanauer, "Place of Stoning," 319; and C. Wilson, *Holy Sepulchre*, 21.

6. See Acts 6:8–15, 7:54–60.

7. See Fetellus, *Fetellus*, 42; Daniel, *Pilgrimage of the Russian Abbot*, 87; and John of Wurzburg, *Description of the Holy Land*, 49.

8. See b. Sanh. 43a.

As a side note, as stated before, even if Queen Helena and Bishop Macarius did find an actual cross from the first century at the traditional Calvary, it was probably a relic from the Roman siege of Jerusalem in 70 CE. Indeed, similar finds are still occurring in northwest Jerusalem to this day. For instance, a Roman ballista ball was discovered just a few decades ago underneath the Church of the Holy Sepulcher.[9] Then, in 2016, at a site near the Church of the Holy Sepulcher, archaeologists excavated dozens more ballista balls used by the Romans.[10]

9. Gibson and Taylor, *Beneath the Church*, 17.

10. See Rabinowitz, "Battle Site," para. 3.

28

Gehenna

Gehenna means the Valley of Hinnom in Aramaic, and it is first mentioned in the Bible in the same verse that introduces Bible Hill.[1] Jesus talks about Gehenna eleven times in the Gospels, indicating the Hinnom Valley was very important to him.[2] (By contrast, Jesus never mentions any landmark around the traditional Calvary even once.) As stated before, following the Babylonian siege of Jerusalem, the Valley of Hinnom was associated with sin, defilement, and divine punishment. In that light, if Bible Hill is Golgotha, then logic suggests Jesus emphasized the dangers of the Hinnom Valley because he wanted to juxtapose the saving power of his sacrifice on Bible Hill with the eternal punishment that awaited unrepentant sinners down below in Gehenna. If this is the case, then the apostles would have surely discerned this unique geographical juxtaposition as they viewed both Calvary and Gehenna from Mount Zion in the months following Jesus' sacrifice on the cross. It is no wonder then that James the Just, who, according to tradition, lived continuously in the Cenacle during the Apostolic Age, cites the dangers of "Gehenna" of all places in his letter to the Judeo-Christians of the diaspora.[3]

1. See Josh 15:8.
2. See Staples, "What Is Hell?," para. 26.
3. See Jas 3:6; and Papaioannou, *Geography of Hell*, 22.

As a side note, according to Josephus, somewhere in northwest Jerusalem (not far from the tomb of John Hyrcanus), the First and Second Walls of the city met at a gate called Gennath. Scholars and theologians usually translate the word Gennath as "garden" because (a) the word for garden in Aramaic sounds like the "Genn" in Gennath, and (b) such a translation supports the hypothesis that Joseph of Arimathea owned a garden tomb at the traditional Calvary. Be that as it may, it is an indisputable fact that the translation of Gennath as "garden" is speculative.[4] If Gennath does not mean garden, however, what does it mean? To answer this, one must turn to Gehenna. In his writings, Josephus apparently never mentions Gehenna even once. This is inconceivable, because the Hinnom Valley is one of the most prominent natural landmarks in the Holy City. This is why the word Gennath is likely an inaccurate transliteration of Gehenna (pronounced "Gehennath" in Jerusalem's local dialect).[5] This makes sense because, unlike the word "garden," the term Gehenna has no equivalent word or expression in Greek, which would have forced Josephus to transliterate it without an accompanying interpretation. How does all this raise the probability of Bible Hill being Golgotha, however? It raises the probability because, if the Gennath Gate was named after the Hinnom Valley, it would further undercut the hypothesis that Joseph of Arimathea owned a garden tomb in northwest Jerusalem. It is also notable that, according to Colonel Claude Conder, "Hinnom" could mean "prince" in the old Canaanite language of the Jebusites.[6] If this is correct (and if Bible Hill is Golgotha), it means Jesus walked across the "Valley of the Prince" to Calvary. This is relevant because one of the titles for Jesus in Scripture is the "Prince of Peace."[7]

4. See Birch, "City of David," 81; Birch, "Zion, the City of David," 180; and Conder and Conder, *Handbook*, 349.

5. See Birch, "Zion, the City of David," 180.

6. Conder, *City of Jerusalem*, 28.

7. See Isa 9:6.

29

Hideout of the Apostles

THE GOSPELS DO NOT reveal where the apostles were hiding during the trial and crucifixion of Jesus. Scripture and tradition, however, provide clues. For instance, according to the Gospel of John, one of the disciples was lurking around Golgotha during Jesus' crucifixion and even approached the cross just before Jesus died.[1] If this disciple was one of the Twelve as tradition maintains, then it makes sense that the apostles must have been holing up somewhere near Golgotha. Where could this hiding place have been? If Bible Hill is Calvary, the answer could be the southwest corner of Gehenna. To be sure, the chief priests and elders would have steered clear of this area of the valley to avoid becoming ritually defiled for Passover.[2] The puritanical Essene extremists called the Herodians would have avoided the area for similar reasons.[3] Because a large sewer line released wastewater from Mount Zion into the southwest corner of Gehenna when Jesus was crucified, both the Romans and the Passover pilgrims would have also left this part of Gehenna alone to avoid its foul stench.[4] What's more, according to tradition, the southwest corner of Gehenna was in the valley below

1. See John 19:26.
2. See John 18:28.
3. See Ben-Daniel, *Mount Arbel*, 18; and Joan Taylor, *Essenes*, 109–30.
4. See Pixner, "'Essene Gate' Area," 96–97.

Caiaphas's mansion and the house of John Mark. If this tradition is correct (and if the apostles were hiding beneath the Shoulder of Hinnom), it means once Peter denied Jesus and left Caiaphas's mansion, he could have carried fresh supplies from John Mark's house down to Gehenna to share with the other apostles, thus bolstering the assumption that the apostles would have been hiding in the Hinnom Valley.[5] The proximity of the southwest corner of Gehenna to Bible Hill would also explain (if Bible Hill is Calvary) how one of the apostles could have suddenly come out of hiding and appeared at the cross.[6] Of course, it would have been dangerous for this apostle to have been climbing up the Shoulder of Hinnom to reach Golgotha, but according to tradition, he was young and strong enough to have done it.[7] At this point, it is extremely important to stress that the traditional hideout of the apostles is less than a quarter mile east of the one proposed here.[8] While the traditional hideout of the apostles makes little sense if Jesus was crucified at the traditional Calvary, it would make perfect sense if Bible Hill is Golgotha. Perhaps this means the traditional hideout of the apostles is rooted in actual history. Indeed, if Gethsemane was in the King's Garden, the apostles could have immediately fled into Gehenna following Jesus' arrest.

Since no academic consensus exists regarding the identity of the disciple who approached Jesus' cross, this book takes the traditional position and assumes it was John Zebedee.[9] If this is accurate, then evidence suggests John got away with approaching the cross because he was a blood relative of Jesus whose presence would have therefore been expected at Calvary, and he was too young to pose a significant threat to the Roman troops at the cross.[10] It is also logical to assume a rock scarp separated Jesus

5. See Matt 26:75.

6. See John 19:26.

7. See Cary and Cary, "Christ's Disciples," 3–12.

8. See Hrimat, "Monastery of St. Onuphrius," para. 4.

9. See Charlesworth, *Beloved Disciple*, 127.

10. See Culpepper, *John the Son of Zebedee*, 63–65; and Wenham, "Relatives of Jesus," 15.

from John, further explaining how John could get close enough to the cross to communicate with Jesus without posing a security threat. (The steep scarp by the apse of today's St. Andrew's Memorial Church on Bible Hill is illustrative in this regard.) John was also one of the boldest and most aggressive of the apostles, which is why Jesus called him a "son of thunder." It makes sense therefore that John the "Son of Thunder" Zebedee would have thrown caution to the wind to approach the cross at Calvary.

The Traditional Hideout of the Apostles as Seen from the Shoulder of Hinnom[11]

11. "Scenic View of the Valley of Hinnom (Courtesy of the American Colony)," photo by Eric Matson, Jan. 7, 1910. National Photo Collection of Israel, public domain.

30

The Geography of Elijah

TRADITION SAYS, AFTER FLEEING from Queen Jezebel, the prophet Elijah rested at a spot around two miles south of Bible Hill.[1] If this is accurate, then perhaps he chose this spot to rest because—as Felix Fabri (on pilgrimage ca. 1483 CE), the Anonymous Spanish Franciscan (on pilgrimage ca. 1550 CE), the Hebrew Bible, and the Jewish haggadah all confirm—Elijah was possibly born there.[2] With that in mind, also recall that, in Jewish tradition, Elijah plays a central role in the Passover meal as the harbinger of the messiah.[3] It is not certain whether this tradition connecting Elijah with the Passover Seder extends back to the first century. However, given that John the Baptist calls Jesus the "Lamb of God," the apostle Paul calls Jesus the "Passover Lamb," and the Gospels mention "Elijah" while Jesus suffered on the cross as the "Lamb of God" during "Passover," logic suggests it does extend back to the time of Jesus in one form or another.[4] As a result, if Bible Hill is Calvary, when the browbeaters at Golgotha exclaimed, "Behold! Jesus calls

1. See Wilson and Lane-Poole, *Picturesque Palestine*, 122. This spot is Conder's Arimathea (see chapter 32 of this book, "Arimathea").

2. Fabri, *Wanderings*, 542–43; and Anonymous Spanish Franciscan, *Rome to Jerusalem*, 25. See also Hirsch et al., "Elijah," 122.

3. See Matt, *Becoming Elijah*, 128–46.

4. See 1 Cor 5:7.

Elijah!" what they probably meant was "Let's see if our famous prophet from down the road comes to save 'Christ' from God's wrath!" On top of that, because tradition says John the Baptist grew up near Bible Hill, and Jesus called John the Baptist "Elijah," perhaps the browbeaters were insulting Jesus on an even deeper level than the above interpretation presents.

As a side note, in the opinion of the prominent biblical scholar N. T. Wright, the apostle Paul went to Arabia after his conversion to the Way because he saw himself as following in the footsteps of Elijah.[5] If this is correct (and if Jesus was crucified in the vicinity of where Elijah grew up), perhaps the connection between Elijah's old stomping ground and Calvary heightened Paul's zeal for Jesus.

5. See Wright, "Paul, Arabia, and Elijah," 683–92. The "Way" refers to the early Christian movement during the Apostolic Age (see Acts 24:14).

31

The Temple Veil

THE LOCATION OF BIBLE Hill overlooking all the routes into southwest Jerusalem gives the site great strategic importance.[1] As a result, militaries have sought to occupy Bible Hill throughout history. To be certain, according to Dr. Gabriel Barkay, a fortress likely stood on the northern side of Bible Hill dating to the ancient kings of Judah.[2] In 63 BCE, Pompey the Great encamped on Bible Hill as part of his strategy to attack the Holy City.[3] In 70 CE, General Titus garrisoned troops on Bible Hill.[4] Between 70 and 300 CE, the X Roman Legion was stationed on Bible Hill.[5] In the 1500s, the Ottoman Turks built a citadel on Bible Hill called Fort Gazelle.[6] In World War I, Bible Hill became the headquarters of the division commander of British forces in Jerusalem.[7] In the 1960s, the Israel Defense Force built a clandestine observation post at Bible Hill.[8]

1. See Barkay, *Ketef Hinnom*, 10.

2. See Barkay et al., "Iron Age Fortress," 67; and Barkay, "Riches of Ketef Hinnom," 31.

3. See Josephus, *War* 5.506.

4. Josephus, *War* 5.504–507.

5. See Barkay, *Ketef Hinnom*, 15.

6. See Barkay, *Ketef Hinnom*, 11.

7. See Oren Cohen Group, "Mount Zion Hotel," para. 11.

8. See Rosovsky, "In Jerusalem of the 1800s," 34.

In view of the above, as a former military commander, odds are Pontius Pilate would have also discerned the tactical importance of Bible Hill and maintained some sort of permanent military presence on the Shoulder of Hinnom accordingly.[9] This boosts the probability that a centurion with a platoon of troops would have been on Bible Hill on the day Jesus was crucified. What's more, if Bible Hill is Calvary, then it may be assumed that, when Jesus died on the cross, the centurion and his troops at Golgotha would have seen the sentries on Mount Zion inexplicably going back and forth to the Temple (to see the ripped temple veil) and correlated the unusual commotion with the earthquake and other unsettling events surrounding the crucifixion of Jesus.[10] It is also conceivable (if Bible Hill is Calvary) that the centurion (along with a contingent of troops under his command) even left Bible Hill to see the ripped temple veil with his own eyes.[11] To be sure, since the Gospel of Matthew is the only Gospel to report the centurion reacting to the death of Jesus simultaneously with his soldiers, this scene could be unique, having occurred after the centurion and his men had already gone to see the ripped temple veil in person. Moreover, if the centurion went to see the ripped temple veil, his absence at Calvary could explain why he is not mentioned in the Gospel of John when a unit of soldiers (on Pilate's orders) leaves the Praetorium for Golgotha to break the legs of the crucifixion victims.[12]

As a side note, if the northern side of Bible Hill was fortified when Jesus was crucified, it would explain why Scripture says the guards were sitting down while Jesus was on the cross.[13] In

9. See Demandt, *Pontius Pilate*, 48.

10. It is also possible the ripped temple veil in the Gospels is simply a metaphor for the body of Jesus as indicated in the Epistle to the Hebrews, where it states Christians can enter the Temple through the veil of Jesus' body. See Heb 10:20. If the torn temple veil is a metaphor, it would certainly explain why the veil of the Temple rips at different times depending on which Gospel one reads.

11. See Matt 27:54.

12. See John 19:32.

13. See Matt 27:36.

short, the fortified walls, palisades, and rock scarps surrounding the northern side of Bible Hill would have provided the guards with ample protection from the multitudes below on the Road of the Patriarchs, allowing Pilate's men to relax a little while on duty (to gamble for Jesus' tunic, for instance). It is also logical to assume that, if the centurion left Calvary to see the ripped temple veil, he would have put his executive officer (called the *optio* in Latin) in charge until he returned.[14]

Soldiers at Bible Hill Monitoring the Shoulder of Hinnom[15]

14. See Webster, *Roman Imperial Army*, 117.

15. "Church Parade of St. Andrews Church by the 1st Ba.[?] The Argyll & Sutherland Highlanders on May 26, '40. Highlanders Arriving on the Church Grounds," photo by Matson photo service, May 26, 1940. Matson photograph collection, U.S. Library of Congress, used with permission.

32

Arimathea

THE PREEMINENT BRITISH ROYAL engineer and surveyor Colonel Claude Conder placed the hometown of Joseph of Arimathea within the modern district of Ramat Rahel on his 1889 map called "Palestine in the Beginning of the Christian Era." According to Conder, Joseph's hometown was located roughly three miles south of Jerusalem, just off the Road of the Patriarchs. The Colonel does not explain why he identified this site as Joseph's hometown. However, his logic may have been guided by the following evidence:

1. Arimathea is a Greek transliteration of the Hebrew word *Ha-Ramathaim*, which means "two heights" or "twin peaks."[1] It so happens Col. Conder's site for Arimathea is located between two similarly sized hills called the Hill of Rachel and the Hill of Elijah. On this basis alone, Conder's site for Joseph's hometown (with its "two heights") could have been called Arimathea in the time of Jesus.

2. According to the Pilgrim of Piacenza (on pilgrimage ca. 570 CE), Conder's Arimathea was called Ramah in antiquity.[2] This is relevant to Conder's Arimathea because, according to the

1. See McClintock and Strong, "Arimathea," para. 1; and McClintock and Strong, "Ramathaimzophim," para. 2.

2. Pilgrim of Piacenza, *Antoninus Martyr*, 23.

Bible, the names *Ramah* and *Arimathea* are interchangeable (as long as the place called Ramah is also a place with two heights). This means the Pilgrim of Piacenza's Ramah could have been called Arimathea as well.[3] This is key evidence for the authenticity of Conder's Arimathea because, in the Old Syriac Gospels (ca. 200 CE), Joseph's hometown is always called Ramah, never Arimathea. Likewise, in the traditions of the Assyrian Church of the East, Joseph is always called Joseph of Ramah, never Joseph of Arimathea.[4] So, the fact that Conder's Arimathea could have been called both Ramah and Arimathea in the time of Jesus not only rationalizes the two names for Joseph's hometown in the Greek and Syriac traditions but also boosts the odds that Conder's Arimathea and the Pilgrim of Piacenza's Ramah both refer to the same town of Arimathea mentioned in the New Testament.

3. According to the Gospel of Matthew, the spirit of the Jewish matriarch Rachel was weeping in the vicinity of Bethlehem at a town called Ramah.[5] This means the Pilgrim of Piacenza's Ramah could be both the Ramah where Rachel wept in the Gospel of Matthew, and the town called Arimathea where Joseph was from. This is because the Pilgrim of Piacenza's Ramah is in the vicinity of Bethlehem where the spirit of Rachel wept at Ramah, and because the names Ramah and Arimathea are interchangeable as long as the place called Ramah is also a place with two heights like Conder's Arimathea.

4. According to several Christian traditions, Conder's Arimathea is (a) where Mary and Joseph rested on their way to Bethlehem before the magi met King Herod in Jerusalem; (b) where the magi saw the Star of Bethlehem after they departed King Herod to find the Holy Family in Bethlehem; and (c) where the Holy Family replenished their water supply as they

3. McClintock and Strong, "Arimathea," para. 1; and McClintock and Strong, "Ramathaimzophim," para. 2.

4. Crawford, "St. Joseph and Britain," 12.

5. See Matt 2:16–18.

fled King Herod's assassins who were coming from Jerusalem to kill Jesus in Bethlehem (as a result of the magi's earlier visit to King Herod).[6] These traditions are important to note because they further correlate Conder's Arimathea with the spirit of Rachel weeping in Ramah via the Massacre of the Innocents.

5. Because tradition holds that the Gospel of Matthew was originally written in Hebrew for first-century Jews, it stands to reason that if Conder's Arimathea is both the hometown of Joseph of Arimathea and the Ramah where the spirit of Rachel wept near Bethlehem, then most of the Jews reading the original Hebrew Gospel of Matthew would have known that Rachel's Ramah and Joseph's Arimathea referred to the same town north of Bethlehem, explaining why the Gospel of Matthew did not clarify this point of geography to its readers.

6. In 330 CE, Eusebius located the tomb of the Jewish matriarch Rachel (whose spirit wept in the vicinity of Bethlehem at Ramah) one mile south of Conder's Arimathea.[7] Yet, in 388 CE, Jerome located Rachel's tomb two miles south of Conder's Arimathea.[8] In view of this southerly drift, logic suggests Rachel's tomb could have originally been located in the vicinity of Conder's Arimathea.[9] This inference is buttressed by the Pilgrim of Piacenza, who said Rachel's tomb was, indeed, situated at Conder's Arimathea.[10] This is relevant to Joseph's hometown because it further correlates the Jewish matriarch

6. See Pilgrim of Piacenza, *Antoninus Martyr*, 23; Pixner, *Messiah*, 46–48; and Theodosius, *Theodosius*, 17.

7. See Joan Taylor, *Onomasticon*, 49.

8. See Joan Taylor, *Onomasticon*, 49.

9. See Schwarz, *Descriptive Geography*, 109–10.

10. Pilgrim of Piacenza, *Antoninus Martyr*, 23. Additionally, according to the esteemed nineteenth century translator and scholar James E. Hanauer, one Greek Orthodox tradition says Conder's Arimathea is the place where Rachel died in childbirth (*Walks*, 245). If this is correct, it also bolsters the contention that Rachel's tomb must have been near Conder's Arimathea.

Rachel (whose spirit wept in Ramah) with both the Pilgrim of Piacenza's Ramah and Conder's Arimathea.

7. According to the Gospel of Luke, Joseph's hometown was in Judea.[11] This is relevant because Conder's Arimathea would have been squarely in Judea in the time of Jesus.
8. If Arimathea was at Conder's site, then Matt 27:57 could be interpreted as saying Joseph had literally walked to Calvary from Arimathea when he saw Jesus on the cross. As will be shown below, such a literal interpretation of this verse would make perfect sense if Bible Hill is Calvary and Conder's Arimathea is Joseph's hometown.

In light of the above (if Conder's Arimathea is the historical hometown of Joseph of Arimathea, and if Bible Hill is Golgotha), then logic suggests the moment Joseph of Arimathea saw Jesus on the cross (prompting him to bury Jesus in his own tomb), he was passing by Bible Hill on his way to Jerusalem from his country estate in Arimathea. This makes sense because, if Joseph had been in Jerusalem all day, he would have likely decided to bury Jesus much earlier (and made arrangements with Pilate accordingly).[12] Given that Joseph was a member of the Sanhedrin, he would have likely entered the Praetorium through the Judgment Gate. No matter how he entered, however, the Bible attests that Pilate responded promptly to Joseph's request for an audience. The direct line of sight between Bible Hill and the Praetorium would also explain how Pilate so swiftly signaled his centurion at Calvary to come and confirm Jesus' death as reported in the Gospel of Mark. Once Pilate verified the death of Jesus (around 4:15 p.m.), Scripture says the governor gave Joseph permission to bury Jesus' body. At this point, Joseph would have still been in a hurry to complete the burial before sundown. As Scripture reports, not only was the Sabbath fast approaching, but Joseph still had to go into the city, buy linen cloth, load it up, return to Golgotha, take Jesus' body

11. See Luke 23:51.

12. Joseph must have returned to Arimathea in disgust after the morning trial of Jesus.

down from the cross, and bury it in his tomb. As long as Joseph hustled, he could have returned to Bible Hill on foot by 5:30 p.m. It would have taken him (and Nicodemus) another ten or fifteen minutes to move Jesus' body from the cross to his tomb (about 170 yards south of the cross). As a rich man, however, logic strongly suggests Joseph of Arimathea would have been riding a horse around Jerusalem, speeding up the timeline considerably. Either way, placing Jesus' body within Joseph's tomb before the sun set would have been difficult, just as Scripture describes. In that context, if Conder's Arimathea is really Joseph's hometown, and if Bible Hill is Golgotha, then, as long as Joseph left Arimathea by 3:00 p.m. when Scripture says the sun came out, the geography of Arimathea, Calvary, and the Praetorium aligns perfectly with the accounts of Jesus' crucifixion in the Bible.

Conder's 1889 Map Identifying Ramat Rahel as the Site of Arimathea[13]

13. "Palestine in the Beginning of the Christian Era," Claude R. Conder, 1889. In Conder, *Palestine*, v.

33

Nicodemus

NICODEMUS WAS AN EXTREMELY wealthy and politically powerful Galilean who was a member of the Sanhedrin in Jerusalem at the time of Jesus' crucifixion.[1] Because the hometowns of Jesus and Nicodemus were both in the suburbs of Sepphoris (i.e., the capital of Galilee), both men would have shared a common attachment to that region of Israel and must have spoken similar dialects of Aramaic.[2] It was to Nicodemus that Jesus revealed the key to eternal life early in his ministry, and it was Nicodemus who helped Joseph of Arimathea entomb Jesus at Golgotha on the day of Jesus' crucifixion.[3]

Both literary and archaeological evidence indicate that, in the time of Jesus, most of the wealthy elites in Jerusalem resided on the western hill of the city.[4] This suggests the mansion of Nicodemus would have been less than a mile from Bible Hill.[5] This detail is

1. See Ochser and Kohler, "Nicodemus," 299–300.

2. Safrai, *Beginnings of Christianity*, 305.

3. See John 3:15, 19:31–40.

4. See Bohstrom, "Priestly Quarters," paras. 1–8; Broshi, "Excavations on Mount Zion," 81–88; and Reed, "Excavating at Mt. Zion," paras. 1–8.

5. According to the Second Anonymous Pilgrim (on pilgrimage ca. 1100 CE), Nicodemus was buried on Mount Zion by the Cenacle. See the Second Anonymous Pilgrim, "Anonymous Pilgrim II," 8.

salient because, according to Scripture, the Sabbath was fast approaching when Joseph of Arimathea saw Jesus on the cross, and it is unlikely that Nicodemus would have transported seventy-five pounds of expensive spices to Golgotha before Pilate gave Joseph permission to entomb Jesus' body. So, time would have been of the essence for Nicodemus when he began his trek to Calvary. No matter where Nicodemus lived exactly on the western hill, however (if Bible Hill is Golgotha), he would have reached Calvary before sunset even if he was carrying the spices by hand. To be certain, contrary to common perception, nothing in Scripture says Nicodemus was old, feeble, or incapable of carrying a heavy load by hand.[6] All this sustains the premise that Bible Hill is Golgotha because it shows that, when one assumes Bible Hill is Calvary, the movement of Nicodemus from Jerusalem to Golgotha harmonizes with Scripture perfectly.

6. See Driscoll, "Nicodemus," para. 1.

34

Calvary and the Bronze Serpent of Moses

According to Scripture, the place where the residents of Jerusalem venerated the bronze serpent of Moses during the Iron Age was likely somewhere outside the Holy City near the high places and sacred pillars such as Bible Hill and Absalom's Monument.[1] This means Bible Hill could be the place where the bronze serpent of Moses was once venerated. This is notable because, early in his ministry, Jesus told Nicodemus that the Son of Man would be lifted up like the bronze serpent of Moses to give eternal life to those who believe in him.[2] Since the "Son of Man" is a title Jesus frequently called himself, and since Bible Hill could be where the bronze serpent of Moses was once venerated, then, if Bible Hill is Golgotha, it is conceivable that Jesus was crucified where this bronze serpent of Moses had, in earlier times, been lifted up for veneration outside the Holy City. This would explain why the sight of Jesus being hung on the cross inspired Nicodemus to start honoring Jesus openly.[3] It would also help account for Jesus being identified as the New Moses following the crucifixion.[4]

1. See 2 Kings 18:1–4.
2. See John 3:14.
3. See John 19:39–40.
4. See Allison, *New Moses*, 261.

35

The Garden Tomb

AN ANCIENT ROCK-HEWN TOMB on the southern slope of Bible Hill is located 170 yards from the area where Jesus would have been crucified near Cave 34 (if Bible Hill is Calvary).[1] Based on the artifacts found in this tomb, it must have been constructed between 25 BCE and 62 CE. As the tomb contained a coin from one of the Roman prefects/procurators, this sepulcher was unquestionably used during the New Testament period.[2] Moreover, the Herodian lamps

1. Because British mandate map-coordinates are estimates based on archival descriptions, the sepulcher on the southern slope of Bible Hill could be Tomb 14–4 or Tomb 14–5 in Kloner and Zissu's book on the Necropolis of Jerusalem (see Kloner and Zissu, *Necropolis*, 359). The tomb on Bible Hill is most likely Tomb 14–4 (as per email correspondence with Dr. Zissu). However, since Tomb 14–5 was hewn in the first century before 70 CE and its layout fits the Gospels, it makes no difference which one of these two tombs is the one on Bible Hill. They both match Scripture. (The other tomb is located around 430 yards south of the northern slope of Bible Hill under a small grocery store across from the Hill of Evil Counsel.)

2. See Rahmani, *Jewish Ossuaries*, 88. The coin was worn nearly flat, so its precise age is unknown. However, because (a) Porcius Festus was the last Roman governor of Jerusalem to mint coins and (b) the last year Porcius Festus minted coins was 59 CE, logic dictates the tomb on the southern slope of Bible Hill could not have been hewn much later than 59 CE (see Wacks, *Biblical Numismatics*, 47). Interestingly, it was Porcius Festus who talked with the apostle Paul in the book of Acts (see Acts 26:24).

in the tomb could date to the early first century, as this type of lamp was manufactured in Palestine between 25 BCE and 150 CE.[3]

While this tomb does not have a diagram of its layout, according to Dr. Levi Rahmani, it was a single-chambered loculi tomb.[4] Kloner and Zissu add that "[its] walls . . . were partially destroyed."[5] It is evident this sepulcher was owned by someone wealthy like Joseph of Arimathea because (when it was excavated) it contained many chip-carved ossuaries, which were elaborately decorated with whirl-rosettes and other beautiful motifs.[6] What's more, assuming Jesus was crucified on the northern slope of Bible Hill, it would have remained ritually pure during the crucifixion of Jesus and yet been close enough to the crucifixion site for Joseph and Nicodemus to have carried Jesus' body there quickly as Scripture describes.[7] Likewise, because this tomb sits about eighty yards from the Road of the Patriarchs, it would explain why the two Marys had to leave the main roadway to see exactly where Joseph and Nicodemus entombed Jesus' body.[8] Its relative seclusion would have caused the chief priests to have worried about its security as well. This would explain why they would have insisted on having soldiers posted outside this tomb as Scripture attests.[9]

It is also relevant that, in the time of Jesus, crucifixions would have been the exception for executions in Jerusalem, not the rule.[10] To be sure, between the death of King Herod in 4 BCE and the Roman siege of Jerusalem in 70 CE, only two explicit cases of crucifixion in the Holy City are reported by Josephus, one of which is the crucifixion of Jesus.[11] (This would explain why the crucifixion

3. See Milwaukee Public Museum, "Pottery Lamps," para. 20.

4. Rahmani, *Jewish Ossuaries*, 88.

5. Kloner and Zissu, *Necropolis*, 359.

6. See Rahmani, *Jewish Ossuaries*, 88.

7. See John 19:38–42.

8. See Matt 27:61.

9. See Matt 27:65.

10. See Gibson, *Final Days*, loc. 83.

11. The first case is Jesus. The second is the salvo of crucifixions by Florus. A third possible case involves the executions in Jerusalem by Albinus. See also

of Jesus was so shocking and memorable.) Plus, if Bible Hill was the Place of Beheading and Strangulation, then even the regular executions on the Shoulder of Hinnom would have occurred by Cave 34—well out of sight of the southern slope of Bible Hill. Moreover, the winds in Jerusalem almost always blow west, which would have carried any scent of decomposition around Cave 34 away from the southern slope of Bible Hill. In addition, first-century glass bottles for pouring perfume and oil have been excavated on the northern slope of Bible Hill, indicating steps were taken to prevent odors from emanating from the tombs there in the first place.[12] Furthermore, pursuant to the Law of Moses, capital punishment was righteous in the eyes of God.[13] If Bible Hill is Calvary, surely Joseph would have considered all this when building a new tomb on the southern slope of Bible Hill. Apart from that, with its exquisite views and proximity to the city, land on the Shoulder of Hinnom would have been at a premium in the time of Jesus no matter what, making it an excellent site in which to invest.[14] Additionally, if King David erected a monument over the skull of Goliath on the Shoulder of Hinnom, making executions there a patriotic spectacle where the heads of more enemies of Israel could join Goliath's, it may be assumed that the legacy of this prestigious monument would have offset the stigma normally attached to other execution sites in Jerusalem.[15] Besides, as someone who worked with the likes of Caiaphas on a regular basis, logic suggests that (despite being a secret disciple of Jesus) Joseph of Arimathea was no saint before the resurrection and would have allowed Roman soldiers to operate on his land in exchange for political favors.[16] This would certainly explain why the Gospel of Peter says Joseph and Pontius Pilate were friends.[17] It would also explain why

Rousseau and Arav, *Jesus and His World*, 74.

12. See Barkay, "Slope of the Hinnom Valley," 99.

13. See Deut 21:21.

14. See Gibson, *Final Days*, loc. 130.

15. See Tenz, "Calvary," 190.

16. See Bond, *Historical Jesus*, 165.

17. See Gibson, *Final Days*, loc. 131.

Joseph would have been willing to abandon his old family tomb in Arimathea for a new, more elite sepulcher on the prestigious Shoulder of Hinnom where he could more prominently display his family's wealth and status.

While there was no ossuary with the name "Joseph" inscribed on it in this tomb on the southern slope of Bible Hill, this should come as no surprise. According to the Gospel of Nicodemus (ca. 350 CE), Joseph was imprisoned by the Jews for entombing Jesus.[18] Also, according to tradition, Joseph of Arimathea traveled to Great Britain as one of the seventy apostles.[19] These later legends suggest Joseph of Arimathea became a target of persecution in Jerusalem for entombing Jesus and would have therefore been motivated to leave Palestine soon after the crucifixion to exert his influence elsewhere to spread the gospel.[20] This assumption is reinforced by the fact that, unlike Nicodemus, no one named Joseph of Arimathea appears anywhere in the writings of Josephus. Plus, according to Eusebius (writing ca. 314 CE), some of the apostles sailed across the ocean as far as the British Isles (where tradition ultimately places Joseph of Arimathea).[21] In that light, as Major-General Charles Wilson contends, following the crucifixion, Joseph of Arimathea likely left Jerusalem "as a missionary to the Gentiles . . . [and for this reason] it is probable, if not certain, that . . . he sold his property, including the garden and tomb, for the benefit of the common purse."[22] After all, Jesus did advise all his disciples to store up treasure in heaven, not on earth.

Even if Joseph did not sell off his property but bequeathed it to his relatives instead, the ossuaries found in the tomb on the southern slope of Bible Hill still conform to what one would expect from the family of Joseph of Arimathea. After all, according to the Gospels, Joseph of Arimathea was a prominent member of the Sanhedrin and had lots of money. This elegant rock-hewn tomb

18. See Toy and Kohler, "Joseph of Arimathea," 256.

19. See Toy and Kohler, "Joseph of Arimathea," 256.

20. See Gibson, *Final Days*, loc. 133.

21. See Eusebius, *Gospels*, 130.

22. C. Wilson, *Holy Sepulchre*, 74.

on the southern slope of Bible Hill full of expensive chip-carved ossuaries is precisely the type of tomb Joseph of Arimathea would have given his relatives. Moreover, according to the Gospel of Matthew, the Jews believed the resurrection of Jesus was a fraud.[23] So, the continued use of this tomb (rather than its veneration) on the southern slope of Bible Hill in the years following the crucifixion actually boosts the probability of it being the historical sepulcher of Joseph of Arimathea.

It is also salient to note that gardens have been cultivated around Bible Hill since at least the first century.[24] It stands to reason therefore that the tomb on the southern slope of Bible Hill would have been surrounded by gardens in the time of Jesus. This observation is relevant because, according to Scripture, the sepulcher of Joseph of Arimathea was a garden tomb. On that note, according to the Targum Neofiti, one of the names for the valley where Abraham met Melchizedek was the "Valley of the Gardens."[25] If this is correct (and if Bible Hill is where Abraham met Melchizedek and where Jesus was crucified), then the burial of Jesus took place in a "garden tomb" in the "Valley of the Gardens." With that in mind, it is worth reiterating that Bible Hill could also be the royal "Garden of Uzza".

It is also pertinent to mention that two of the four rolling-stone tombs from the first century in Jerusalem are only a quarter mile north of Bible Hill.[26] This indicates the blocking stone for the sepulcher on the southern slope of Bible Hill could have plausibly been a rolling stone or a square stone, increasing the chances of Bible Hill being Golgotha. It is also notable that, because Lady Mary had relatives in Bethlehem through her marriage to Joseph, these relatives would have likely possessed family tombs near Bethlehem where she could have permanently buried her son in accordance with Jewish custom. This is relevant because, if Joseph's tomb was

23. See Matt 28:11–15.

24. See Barkay, *Ketef Hinnom*, 11–12; Dunlop, *Faith Rewarded*, 200; Fabri, *Wanderings*, 541; and Josephus, *War* 5.507.

25. See McNamara, "Melchizedek," 3.

26. See Kloner and Zissu, *Necropolis*, 720.

on the southern slope of Bible Hill, its location by the road to Bethlehem would rationalize the verses in Scripture describing the women coming to Joseph's tomb early in the morning on Easter Sunday with spices, as if they were coming there to prepare Jesus' body for permanent burial somewhere else relatively close by.[27]

As a side note, in an effort to refute the resurrection of Jesus, the *Toledot Yeshu* (ca. 150–450 CE) says the body of Jesus was not raised from the dead but was buried by an aqueduct, causing it to be washed away when Pilate flooded the aqueduct with water.[28] The existence of this ancient polemic against the resurrection of Christ in the *Toledot Yeshu* is hard to explain if Jesus was buried at the traditional Calvary. However, if the tomb on the southern slope of Bible Hill belonged to Joseph of Arimathea, then the likely origin of this tale immediately becomes clear. Excavations on the Shoulder of Hinnom reveal that several aqueducts existed there in the time of Jesus.[29] It is conceivable then (if Bible Hill is Golgotha) that the Jews who rejected the idea of Jesus' resurrection in the Apostolic Age looked to the aqueducts at Calvary as an explanation for how the apostles could have made Jesus' body seemingly disappear without a trace from Golgotha. Remarkably, if all this is accurate, it may also explain why Josephus mentions the crucifixion of Jesus right after he recounts an episode where Pontius Pilate punishes a crowd of Jews at the Praetorium for protesting against his new aqueduct. Put simply, writing about Pilate punishing Jews at the Praetorium for opposing his new aqueduct could have triggered Josephus' memory about Jesus also being punished by Pilate and the contested explanations for the disappearance of Jesus' body near the aqueducts on the Shoulder of Hinnom.

27. See Brodrick, *Trial and Crucifixion*, 173; and C. Wilson, *Holy Sepulchre*, 74.

28. See Schmidt, *Josephus and Jesus*, 131–32. The *Toledot Yeshu* reflects some of the earliest known Jewish polemics against Jesus as the Messiah found outside the Gospels.

29. Amit and Gibson, "Water to Jerusalem," 18.

The Southern Slope of Bible Hill[30]

30. "Cityscape with Apartment Building, a Synagogue, and in the Foreground the Remains of a Wall," photo by Willem van de Poll, 1964. Dutch National Archives.

36

The Supermarket Tomb

In 1943, a rock-cut tomb was discovered about 430 yards south of the northern slope of Bible Hill under today's "Super Deal" supermarket. The tomb's shallow standing pit with ledges on three sides, along with other finds, place the tomb's construction squarely in the first century CE.[1] It is also roughly ten feet wide, ten feet long, and six feet high. The door to this tomb was destroyed by construction, so the type of blocking stone it had is unknown. (Even if the blocking stone was square, however, the renowned archaeologist Dr. Amos Kloner has shown how square stones conform to Scripture just as much as disk-shaped ones.)[2] The entrance to this tomb was low as well, forcing people to lean forward to peer inside. This detail is relevant because the entrance to the tomb of Joseph of Arimathea was also low.[3] What's more, though the tomb on the southern slope of Bible Hill remains the best fit for the tomb of Joseph of Arimathea, it is not impossible that the supermarket tomb was, in fact, the actual Holy Sepulcher of Jesus. To be sure, in the time of Jesus, a Sabbath's day journey was somewhere between one thousand and twelve hundred yards,

1. See Kloner and Zissu, *Necropolis*, 359.
2. Kloner, "Rolling Stone," 23.
3. See John 20:5.

and the supermarket tomb is roughly eleven hundred yards from Gabbatha. In that light (if the supermarket tomb is the tomb of Joseph of Arimathea), then the chief priests could have conceivably walked from Gabbatha to the tomb of Joseph of Arimathea to post guards there without exceeding a Sabbath's day journey in the process. Moreover, because the tomb of Joseph of Arimathea could have theoretically been as far away as two miles from the crucifixion site according to the Gospel of John, the 430 yards between the northern slope of Bible Hill and the supermarket tomb does not preclude this tomb from having belonged to Joseph of Arimathea.[4] All this boosts the odds that Bible Hill is Golgotha because it proves that, even if the tomb on the southern slope of Bible Hill did not belong to Joseph of Arimathea, the actual tomb of Christ could have nonetheless been located somewhere else nearby.[5]

4. The Gospel of John says Joseph's tomb was *near* the site of crucifixion (see John 19:42). It also says Bethany was *near* Jerusalem (see John 11:18). Since Bethany was two miles from Jerusalem, logic dictates Joseph's tomb could have been as far away from the crucifixion site as two miles.

5. See J. Chadwick, "Revisiting Golgotha," 41–43, for more insights.

37

Simeon Hillel and Joseph's Tomb

According to writings by Baron d'Anglure (1395), John Poloner (1421), George Sandys (1610), and Henry Maundrell (1697), the prophet Simeon, who held Jesus as an infant in the Temple, had a house near Bible Hill, the ruins of which are currently enclosed within the Orthodox Church of St. Simeon about a mile southwest of the Shoulder of Hinnom.[1] In the opinion of some scholars, this prophet Simeon (who held the infant Jesus) was arguably the same Jewish leader named Simeon Hillel who served on the Sanhedrin in Jerusalem during the reign of Herod the Great.[2] If these two Simeons were really one and the same person, and if the tradition about the location of his house is correct, then it stands to reason Simeon Hillel would have bequeathed his house near the Shoulder of Hinnom to one of his sons such as the famous rabbi Gamaliel (who served on the Sanhedrin with Nicodemus in the time of Jesus). If this was the case, then either Gamaliel or one of Gamaliel's brothers would have likely owned property near Bible Hill when Jesus was crucified.[3] This inference bolsters the premise that other wealthy Jews such as Joseph of Arimathea would have also owned

1. See Pringle, *Crusader Kingdom*, 166–67.

2. See Cutler, "Simeon of Luke," 29; and Marshall, "Simeon in Luke 2," paras. 1–8.

3. See Acts 5:34–39.

property near the Shoulder of Hinnom in the time of Jesus. This in turn buttresses the assertion that the tomb on the southern slope of Bible Hill belonged to Joseph of Arimathea, reinforcing the contention that Bible Hill is the site of Jesus' crucifixion.

38

The Arcosolium of John Hyrcanus

THE LIMESTONE BENCH IN the alleged tomb of Christ in the Church of the Holy Sepulcher is frequently identified as being the base of an arcosolium where, according to tradition, Joseph of Arimathea entombed Jesus' body.[1] However, there is no definitive evidence showing this bench was ever the base of an arcosolium. To be certain, in describing this bench, Eusebius calls it a "lone cavern" within a "cave."[2] This is hardly the description of a luxurious first-century arcosolium designed for a wealthy member of the Sanhedrin like Joseph of Arimathea. Moreover, once the Fatimid Muslims ransacked the traditional Calvary in 1009 CE, any remaining evidence that might have shed significant light on the true origin of this bench was annihilated.[3] Plus, even if this bench was the base of an arcosolium from the Second Temple period, logic suggests it would have belonged to the high priest John Hyrcanus. Certainly, in 2007, an arcosolium dating to the time of John Hyrcanus was excavated twenty miles southwest of Jerusalem. This indicates the tomb of John Hyrcanus could have included

1. See Joan Taylor, "Golgotha," para. 34.
2. C. Wilson, *Holy Sepulchre*, 185.
3. See Gibson and Taylor, *Beneath the Church*, 62.

an arcosolium as well.[4] This fact further undercuts the traditional Calvary, thereby elevating the chances that the tomb on the southern slope of Bible Hill is the actual tomb of Christ.

4. See Greenhut, "Horbat," paras. 23–24.

39

The Pseudo Tomb of Joseph of Arimathea

In the Church of the Holy Sepulcher, there is a room in the Syrian Chapel near the edicule called the Tomb of Joseph of Arimathea. This room is frequently said to contain several ancient Jewish loculi belonging to Joseph of Arimathea. There are several points to be made about the loculi in this room. Firstly, the dimensions of these loculi do not correspond with the typical dimensions of loculi from the time of Jesus.[1] Because of this, some scholars have speculated that these loculi could be pseudo tombs cut by ultra-zealous crusaders.[2] This is not baseless speculation either. As recently as 1810, for instance, a sizeable chunk of the "sacred" Rock of Calvary in the Church of the Holy Sepulcher was intentionally cut away to allow a marble casing to be laid on top of it.[3] Likewise, the present Stone of Anointing in the Church of the Holy Sepulcher is not authentic, but a replica of the original dating to 1810.[4] Even if one assumes these loculi are not medieval forgeries, however, there is still no way of knowing precisely when

1. See Clermont-Ganneau, "So-Called Tomb," 319–27.
2. See Clermont-Ganneau, "So-Called Tomb," 322.
3. C. Wilson, *Ordnance Survey*, 51.
4. See Murphy-O'Connor, *Holy Land*, loc. 55.

they were hewn.[5] They could have been cut out of the rock as early as 100 BCE, for instance, and brought within the confines of the city with the construction of the Second Wall as early as the Hasmonean Dynasty (ca. 140–37 BCE).[6] On top of that, only a few years after the crucifixion, Herod Agrippa was building a massive defensive wall to protect all the new neighborhoods in Bezetha. In that light, when Jesus died on the cross, there is no way the financially astute Joseph of Arimathea would have been investing copious amounts of money in a new sepulcher in northwest Jerusalem where the patently growing population would have ensured its retirement before his own bones could have been laid to rest there.[7] It is highly unlikely, therefore, that these holes in the rock found in the Syrian Chapel of the Church of the Holy Sepulcher ever belonged to Joseph of Arimathea.[8]

5. See J. Chadwick, "Revisiting Golgotha," 15.

6. See Magness, "Jesus and James," 127–28. The historical record does not reveal who built the Second Wall.

7. This is because first-century Jews were never buried inside the walls of a city.

8. See J. Chadwick, "Revisiting Golgotha," 15.

40

Caiaphas's Country Estate

THE MOUNTAIN ACROSS THE street from Bible Hill has been "called by Christians since the fourteenth century 'the Hill of Evil Council' and [is] supposed to have been the site of the country house of Caiaphas, where Judas plotted to betray Christ."[1] Normally, such a late tradition would be taken with a grain of salt. However, an exception should be made in this case because, in 1990, the tomb and ossuary of the high priest Caiaphas were discovered on the southern slope of this Hill of Evil Counsel.[2] Along with the ossuary of the high priest, archaeologists also discovered two Roman-era nails in the tomb. According to research by Shimron, Deutsch, Schoch, and Gutkin, these nails were used to crucify someone.[3] While this does not prove a connection between the nails and the crucifixion of Jesus, it reinforces the possibility of a connection. This inference is bolstered by the fact that, between the death of King Herod in 4 BCE and the Roman siege of Jerusalem in 70 CE, only two explicit cases of crucifixion in Jerusalem are reported by Josephus—one of which is the execution of Jesus. Plus, if Bible Hill is Golgotha, the geography also supports such a connection. After

1. Warren and Conder, *Survey of Western Palestine*, 397. Today this mountain is called Abu Tor.

2. See Bond, *Caiaphas*, 4.

3. Shimron et al., "Petrochemistry," 260.

learning Jesus was dead, for example, it would have been easy for Caiaphas to have walked to Bible Hill, demanded the nails that crucified Jesus, and then walked back to Mount Zion with the nails in his satchel. (He could have ordered a servant to do this for him as well if interacting with the Romans would have defiled him.) Moreover, since Mount Zion is less than a Sabbath day's journey from Bible Hill, it follows that (if Bible Hill is Golgotha), the account in the Gospel of Matthew where the chief priests and Pharisees walk from the Praetorium to Calvary on the Sabbath to secure Jesus' tomb is possible. It would also be plausible because, after leaving guards at the tomb, the chief priests and Pharisees could have stayed at one of their country estates (e.g., the country estate of Caiaphas) near the Shoulder of Hinnom until the Sabbath ended.

As a side note, some critics assert that the nails in Caiaphas's tomb would not have been used in a crucifixion because the wood on the nails has been identified as expensive cedar from Lebanon.[4] These critics say Pilate would have only used cheap wood to crucify his victims.[5] This premise would only make sense, however, if Pilate crucified his victims inconspicuously. Yet, as the Gospels illustrate, under Pilate, crucifixions were public spectacles. This indicates Jesus was crucified on a large Latin-style cross just as tradition maintains. To ensure these large crosses would not disintegrate while in storage or by repeated exposure to the bodily fluids of crucifixion victims, Pilate would have sensibly invested in crosses made of cedar. After all, cedar is a durable wood that naturally resists decay. For this reason, the fact that cedar wood was found on the nails in Caiaphas's tomb does nothing to diminish the odds that these nails were used in a crucifixion. It is also possible that, in the time of Jesus, after arriving from Lebanon cedar wood was carved into crosses in the Valley of the Cross, giving rise to the tradition connecting that valley with the true cross of Jesus.

4. David, "Nails," para. 28.

5. David, "Nails," para. 28.

Bird's Eye View of the Hill of Evil Counsel and Bible Hill[6]

6. "Motorway in Landscape Towards the City," photo by Willem van de Poll, 1964. Copyright Dutch National Archives.

41

Easter Sunday and Bible Hill

When Jesus was crucified, the area around the tomb of John Hyrcanus in northwest Jerusalem was in full view of the Praetorium, the Antonia Fortress, the neighborhoods of Bezetha, and the numerous lookouts standing guard in the towers along the First and Second Walls of the city. As a result, if the tomb of Joseph of Arimathea was really near the tomb of John Hyrcanus (as advocates of the traditional Calvary maintain), then the chief priests' request for added security at Joseph's tomb to prevent Jesus' disciples from stealing Jesus' body becomes patently absurd.[1] A tomb containing the body of Jesus right outside the Praetorium in northwest Jerusalem, for instance, would have been not only under constant surveillance from the towers of Herod's palace, but would have also been continually surrounded by gawking pilgrims, even at night, when the entire area would have been illuminated by the torches along the walls of the Praetorium and the full moon of Passover. Given these conditions, stealing the body of Jesus from a tomb in this part of Jerusalem would have been virtually impossible, with or without increased security at the sepulcher. In that light, adding a guard in this part of the city would have made Caiaphas and Pilate look especially insecure and weak, thereby elevating the

1. See Matt 27:62. See also Reilly, "Mount Calvary," para. 3.

status of Jesus (and his disciples by association) in the eyes of the people. It is extremely unlikely therefore that Caiaphas and Pilate would have commissioned a security detail to guard Joseph's tomb if it had really been located by the tomb of John Hyrcanus. Plus, if Joseph's tomb was in northwest Jerusalem, it would mean that, on Easter morning, Peter and John would have been visibly running through enemy territory where the Herodians, Sadducees, and many of the Pharisees would have been on the hunt for them. This completely flies in the face of Scripture that depicts the apostles, including Peter and John, as *hiding behind locked doors in utter fear* when they come to Jerusalem on Easter Sunday.[2] Indeed, according to the Gospel of Peter, the apostles were in hiding after the crucifixion because they had been accused of plotting to burn down the Temple by the Jewish authorities. If this tradition is accurate, it clearly upholds the assertion that the apostles were nowhere near the tomb of John Hyrcanus following the crucifixion of Jesus, but instead were somewhere farther outside the city where they could monitor their surroundings and evade capture.[3] With this in mind, it seems a new, realistic version of the first Easter Sunday is in order, one in which the apostles are not insanely running around the heart of enemy territory but are cautiously camping in the Rephaim Valley near Bible Hill.

To explain, first consider the Festival of Booths. The Feast of Booths was a seven-day camping festival that took place each year in Jerusalem. Every Jewish male was required to set up a small tent and live in it for a week to recall how the Israelites lived in tents following the Exodus. Since every Jewish male had to camp in a tent in Jerusalem during the Festival of Booths, it stands to reason that Peter, John, and the other apostles not only were capable of camping around the Holy City but also had experience doing so. What's more, according to the Gospel of Peter, the soldiers guarding Jesus' tomb were camping in tents at Calvary. If this tradition is correct, it strengthens the premise that the apostles were camping near Calvary too. Additionally, it is improbable that the apostle John would

2. See John 20:19, 26.

3. See McBirnie, *Authentic Tomb*, 73–74.

have allowed Jesus' mother to sleep in the defiled southwest corner of Gehenna, but would have instead provided a secure place for her near the tomb of Joseph of Arimathea such as a campsite in the Rephaim Valley. Moreover, because the mother of Jesus was staying with John after the crucifixion, if the apostles were camping, odds are the other women (such as Mary Magdalene) would have been camping near the apostles as well. Consider also that, according to tradition (backed by Scripture), Lady Mary had relatives just four miles west of Bible Hill in Ein Karem.[4] If this tradition is accurate (and if the apostles were camping near Bible Hill), then Mary's relatives in Ein Karem could have provided the apostles with vital supplies and helped them flee into the Judean foothills to evade arrest, should the need have arisen.[5] It is also telling that Scripture never reveals where the apostles were sojourning in the time between the crucifixion and the resurrection. This indicates the Eleven were staying somewhere inconspicuous like the Rephaim Valley (rather than somewhere notable like Bethany, or dangerous like the Cenacle). Plus, camping in the Rephaim Valley would have been perfectly normal at Passover. As Dr. James D. Tabor explains, "[during Passover] the thousands of pilgrims [in Jerusalem] stayed with friends, relatives, or in outdoor camps crammed around the outskirts of the walled city, crowding the nearby villages."[6] Furthermore, it is unlikely that the apostles would have been camping near Gordon's Calvary because that area was apparently reserved for Samaritans during Passover.[7]

In light of everything above, consider the merits of the following account of the first Easter Sunday as evidence showing Bible Hill could be Golgotha: Imagine that it is the first Easter morning nearly two thousand years ago. The apostles and women are camping about half a mile west of Bible Hill. Since it is Sunday, there are no restrictions on the distance Jews can travel. As a result, Mary Magdalene gets up before dawn, leaves her tent, and heads

4. See Theodosius, *Theodosius*, 10; and Luke 1:39–40.

5. See Gibson, *Cave of John*, 17; and Schick, "Birthplace," 69.

6. Tabor, *Lost Mary*, 29–30.

7. See Schofield, *Where He Dwelt*, 231.

straight to Bible Hill alone to check on Joseph's tomb. She finds Joseph's tomb empty, so she runs to tell Peter and John back at their campsite. (As Mary runs to find Peter and John, someone shuts the tomb again, presumably one of the Roman guards, as they are seen at the tomb a short time later.) Before Mary reaches Peter and John, however, she runs into other women coming to the tomb with spices. Mary Magdalene returns to the tomb with the women where they experience an earthquake, meet two angels, and watch the guards cower in fear. After that, the women flee from the tomb, too terrified and bewildered to say anything to anyone. When they regain their composure a short time later, however, they split up to inform the apostles back at the campsite about the empty tomb (but say nothing about the supernatural events, probably due to a combination of their own disbelief and fear of being mocked.) At once, Mary Magdalene goes to find Peter and John. When she locates them, she tells them about the empty tomb, and says she does not know where "they" (i.e., the Roman guards) have laid Jesus. The two apostles immediately run to Bible Hill to see what is really going on, with Mary right on their heels. They can do this because the Roman guards are still cowering in fear and pose no immediate threat. Peter and John find the tomb empty just as Mary told them. The two apostles soon leave Calvary (to evade capture from the soldiers now awake on the north side of Bible Hill), but Mary stays outside Joseph's sepulcher weeping. At some point, after talking with two angels and the risen Jesus by the empty tomb, Mary also leaves Bible Hill and joins up with Joanna, Salome, and the mother of James. As the ladies walk along toward their campsite, they see Jesus and worship him.

After the women worship Jesus, the chronology of events goes beyond the scope of this particular chapter, save one incident. When the apostles enter Jerusalem later that evening, they are terrified of the authorities and keep the doors of the house they are staying in locked. This is in stark contrast to the behavior of the apostles that morning, which underpins the contention that the apostles were camping in the Rephaim Valley near Bible Hill after the crucifixion, not running around the tomb of John Hyrcanus by the Praetorium in northwest Jerusalem.

Camping Outside the Walls of Jerusalem[8]

8. "Snow in Jerusalem, 1921. Arabs in Tent in Snow," photo by American Colony (Jerusalem), 1921. Matson photograph collection, U.S. Library of Congress, used with permission.

42

The Report of the Guards

AFTER WITNESSING CERTAIN SUPERNATURAL events at Joseph of Arimathea's tomb on Easter morning, some of the guards left Calvary to report what they saw to the chief priests in Jerusalem.[1] If Bible Hill is Golgotha, then the likely movement of these guards can be logically deduced: They would have left Bible Hill, walked across the bridge to Calvary, entered Jerusalem through the Judgment Gate, and finally reported the morning's events to the chief priests in Caiaphas's mansion (where the chief priests would subsequently bribe the guards to spread the lie that the apostles stole the body of Jesus at night).[2] This straightforward inference reinforces the premise that Bible Hill is Golgotha. It is also noteworthy that if the tomb on the southern slope of Bible Hill belonged to Joseph of Arimathea, then the lie spread by the guards would have been plausible in the years immediately following Jesus' crucifixion. This would explain how many of the Jews could be convinced that the resurrection was a fraud.[3] By contrast, as explained before, if the guards had said the apostles successfully body snatched Jesus by the tomb of John Hyrcanus in full view of the thousands of potential witnesses in Bezetha and the Praetorium, they would have been laughed out of town.

1. See Matt 28:11.
2. See Matt 28:12–15.
3. See Matt 28:15.

43

White Garments, Essenes, and Calvary

One of the unique characteristics of the Essenes was the way they wore white clothing to distinguish themselves from other Jews.[1] In view of this, and because an enclave of Essenes likely lived near Bible Hill in the time of Jesus, it stands to reason that Jewish men wearing white garments would have probably been a common sight on the Shoulder of Hinnom when Jesus was crucified.[2] This is relevant to Bible Hill as Golgotha because all the angels who appear in Scripture at Calvary are wearing white garments like Essenes. In fact, in the Gospel of Mark, one of the angels at Golgotha looks so much like an Essene, it would be impossible to know he was not one without reading the other Gospels to clarify the matter. In view of this, the white clothing of the angels at Golgotha could reflect the social geography of the historical Calvary, thus boosting the odds that Bible Hill is Golgotha. After all, the anonymity of ministering angels was a core belief of the early Christians.[3] Consequently, even if the "angels" at Calvary were, in reality, just Essene men wearing white garments, this would not change the fact that early Christians may have nevertheless viewed

1. See Josephus, *War* 2.123.
2. See Ben-Daniel, "Essenes and Jerusalem," 77.
3. See Heb 1:14, 13:2.

these men as heavenly messengers in disguise and described them accordingly in the Gospels. If one believes in the supernatural, however, it is also possible these "angels" were actual heavenly messengers disguised as Essenes. Either way, the white clothing of these mysterious characters is evidence that Bible Hill is Golgotha. (As a side note, according to some scholars, in the time of Jesus, the residents of Bethany on Mount Olivet were also Essenes.[4] This is notable because it could explain why Scripture also reports the angels on Mount Olivet wearing white garments.)[5]

A Scene Reminiscent of the Essenes on the Shoulder of Hinnom[6]

4. See Pixner, *Messiah*, 227–37; and Yadin, *Temple Scroll*, 177.

5. See Acts 1:10.

6. "Lower Pool of Gihon," illustration by William Henry Bartlett, 1846. In Bartlett, *Walks About the City*, 56.

44

The Road to Emmaus

IN THE LATE MORNING or early afternoon of the first Easter Sunday, Jesus met two of his disciples on a road leading to a village located seven miles from Jerusalem called Emmaus.[1] This description of Emmaus is substantiated by Josephus, who also says there was a village called Emmaus roughly seven miles from the Holy City.[2] In that light, it is astonishing that the traditional site of Emmaus is thirty miles from Jerusalem—much too far from the Holy City to complement Scripture.[3] As a result, the historical site of the biblical Emmaus remains unconfirmed to this day.

In 1883, the British explorer Elizabeth Finn identified a potential site for Emmaus seven miles southwest of Jerusalem (and two miles south of Bethlehem) near the Road of the Patriarchs at the modern village called Artas (also spelled Irtas).[4] This is

1. See Luke 24:13. One early manuscript, however, says thirty miles.

2. See Conder and Conder, *Handbook*, 326; and Josephus, *War* 7.217. Some manuscripts of *War* record Emmaus being four miles from Jerusalem, however.

3. See Masterman, "Emmaus," para. 3. While Codex Sinaiticus does report a journey of thirty miles from Jerusalem to Emmaus, this distance does not comport with the narrative of this journey in Scripture. Nor does it agree with the seven-mile distance reported by the other major New Testament codices. See Conder and Conder, *Handbook*, 326.

4. See Masterman, "Emmaus," para. 5.

noteworthy because, if Bible Hill is Calvary (and if the disciples were camping in the Rephaim Valley after the crucifixion), then Finn's site for Emmaus would complement Scripture perfectly, thus boosting the odds that Jesus was crucified on Bible Hill.[5] Certainly, since most of the events in the Old Testament occurred near the Road of the Patriarchs, walking on this road from Jerusalem to Emmaus would have been ideal for discussing "all that the prophets had spoken about the Messiah."[6] Likewise, because the Road of the Patriarchs was a major road leading into Jerusalem in the first century, the two disciples who walked with Jesus to Emmaus could have easily returned to the Holy City before sunset in accordance with Scripture.[7] It is also noteworthy that, according to the Gospel of Mark, Simon of Cyrene was "coming in from the country" while the disciples walking to Emmaus were "going out to the country."[8] This would not be a coincidence if Bible Hill is Calvary, and if Artas is Emmaus.[9] It is also noteworthy (in defense of a southwest location for Emmaus) that the distinguished Col. Conder also located the biblical Emmaus at a site not too far from Finn's Emmaus.[10]

As a side note, in the opinion of some biblical scholars, the names Clopas, Cleopas, and Cleophas are one and the same.[11] This is relevant because, if true, it means Jesus probably walked with his paternal uncle Cleophas (called Cleopas in the Gospel of Luke) from Jerusalem to Emmaus on Easter Sunday.[12] Certainly, given that Jesus' adoptive father Joseph was from Bethlehem, it makes sense that his paternal uncle Cleophas could have been living in a village near Bethlehem called Emmaus. Moreover, if Clopas,

5. See Finn, "Emmaus Identified," 58; and Conder, "Emmaus," 700.

6. See Luke 24:25–27.

7. See Finn, "Emmaus Identified," 64.

8. See Mark 15:21, 16:12.

9. The earliest manuscripts of Mark do not include verse 16:12, undercutting the strength of this line of evidence.

10. See Conder and Conder, *Handbook*, 304, 326–27.

11. See Wenham, "Relatives of Jesus," 13.

12. See Bauckham, "Relatives of Jesus," 19.

Cleopas, and Cleophas are the same name, then Mary Clopas, who was at Calvary when Jesus was crucified, was likely Jesus' aunt (the wife of Cleophas) and, therefore, would have been the other disciple walking with Cleophas and Jesus to Emmaus.[13] In that light, (if Bible Hill is Calvary) and if Jesus' Aunt Mary and Uncle Cleophas were camping with the apostles seven miles north of Emmaus near Golgotha during the Sabbath, it would rationally explain how Cleophas knew so much about the empty tomb when he talked with Jesus about it on the road to Emmaus.[14] Before leaving the Rephaim Valley, he would have heard all about it from the women who had seen the empty tomb earlier that day.[15] Plus, it just makes sense that Jesus would have wanted to spend some time with his aunt and uncle that first Easter. It would have been a touching moment for Cleophas and Mary to have seen their nephew, whom they had surely known since he was a little boy, one more time in Emmaus.

Elizabeth Finn's Road to Emmaus[16]

13. See V. Jones, "Mary, Wife of Cleopas," para. 2; and Wright, *Luke for Everyone*, 291–94.

14. See Luke 24:22–24.

15. See Luke 24:9 and Matt 28:8.

16. "Rachel's Tomb," photo by American Colony (Jerusalem), ca. 1898–1946. Matson photograph collection, U.S. Library of Congress, used with permission.

45

Akeldama

THE MADABA MAP (CA. 550 CE) contains the oldest original cartographic depiction of Jerusalem on earth. It is therefore a highly valuable resource for evaluating biblical sites like Akeldama where Judas Iscariot hanged himself. On the Madaba map, Akeldama is positioned in southwest Jerusalem in the Hinnom Valley. What's more, this location for Akeldama is substantiated by the medieval churchmen Adamnan (writing in 670 CE) and Buchard of Mount Zion (on pilgrimage in 1283 CE).[1] This suggests Judas Iscariot met his end below the Shoulder of Hinnom in today's Mitchell Park by the Hebron-Road Bridge. To be sure, according to the Franco-German author Philip J. Baldensperger (who grew up in Jerusalem), local potters in his day collected clay in the Hinnom Valley where Mitchell Park is now located; plus, scores of ancient potsherds have been excavated on the Shoulder of Hinnom.[2] This is relevant because Judas Iscariot hanged himself in a potter's field.[3] The fact that hundreds of foreigners lived in the military

1. See Adamnan, *Arculfus*, 19; and Buchard of Mount Zion, *Description of the Holy Land*, 80. This stone bridge is cited by the Venerable Bede in 705 CE as well. See also Conder, *City of Jerusalem*, 18.

2. Baldensperger, "Immovable East," 136–37.

3. See Matt 27:7.

camp of the Praetorium facing southwest Gehenna in the time of Jesus also bolsters the idea that Judas hanged himself somewhere near there. This is because the chief priests built a cemetery for foreigners at the place where Judas hanged himself.[4] Furthermore, according to Papias (writing ca. 120 CE), the place where Judas killed himself was putrid.[5] This description would make perfect sense if Akeldama had been located near the Praetorium's leach field. Hanging himself in front of the Praetorium for everyone to see would also explain how the entire City of Jerusalem came to know about Judas's demise.[6] The tradition connecting Judas to the country estate of Caiaphas also suggests Judas was familiar with the Shoulder of Hinnom, increasing the odds that he would have hanged himself somewhere in its vicinity. On top of that, the Gospel of Matthew correlates the location of Akeldama with Gehenna through the prophecies of Jeremiah. In this light, if Bible Hill is Golgotha, it makes sense that, as soon as Judas saw Jesus nailed to the cross, he would have realized the gravity of his situation, gone to the Temple to get rid of his blood money, and then shamefully hanged himself in the potter's field in Gehenna near the stone bridge to Calvary (where Jeremiah had centuries earlier stood prophesying the coming destruction of Jerusalem). In any case, all this is relevant to Bible Hill as Golgotha because it ties another major event in the passion of Jesus to southwest Jerusalem.

4. See Matt 27:7.

5. Meyer, *Judas*, 116.

6. See Acts 1:19.

The Field of Blood as Recorded on the Madaba Map[7]

7. "Lower Pool of Gibon," American Colony (Jerusalem) ca. 1900–1920. Matson photograph collection, U.S. Library of Congress, used with permission.

46

The Gate to Hell

According to tradition, the Apostles' Creed was composed in the Cenacle on the day of Pentecost by the twelve apostles.[1] This reflects the great antiquity of the Apostles' Creed.[2] In the Apostles' Creed, Jesus descends into hell after dying on the cross. This is puzzling because no verse in Scripture says anything outright about Jesus visiting hell after the crucifixion. Only a few verses even allude to it.[3] How then did the idea of Jesus visiting hell after his death on the cross become such a core article of faith in early Christianity? Perhaps part of the answer lies in the cultural geography of southwest Jerusalem. According to the Babylonian Talmud, Jerusalem's gate to hell is located in Gehenna.[4] While the Talmud never specifies the exact location of this hell gate in Gehenna, it does correlate its location with Mount Zion.[5] This boosts the odds that it sat somewhere in the southwest corner of the Hinnom Valley between Mount Zion and Bible Hill. This inference is bolstered by the book of First Enoch, according to which the

1. See Thurston, "Apostles' Creed," para. 1
2. See McClintock and Strong, "Creed, Apostles," para. 4
3. See, for instance, 1 Pet 3:18–20.
4. See Kohler and Blau, "Gehenna," 582.
5. See Kohler and Blau, "Gehenna," 582.

valley below Mount Zion is the place where God will judge the eternally damned.[6] Moreover, according to the Talmud, the minister of hell lives in Gehenna where he constantly implores God to feed him more and more souls.[7] What's more, the idea that Jesus preached to the saints in Sheol and the eternally damned in hell after the crucifixion is sustained by the great thirteenth-century theologian Thomas Aquinas.[8] In that light, if Bible Hill is Golgotha (and if Jerusalem's hell gate was below the Shoulder of Hinnom), then it would have been natural for the apostles gazing at Calvary from Mount Zion to assume the Savior of Israel descended into hell through the hell gate below Bible Hill, preached to the spirits in prison, returned to Bible Hill through the same hell gate, and then rose from the dead.[9] This would help explain how the idea of Jesus visiting hell became such a core article of faith in early Christianity.

6. See 1 En. 27:2.
7. See b. Sabb. 104a.
8. See Goris, "Christ's Descent into Hell," 94.
9. See Luke 24:44–47 and 1 Pet 3:18–19.

47

The Tower of the Flock

THE TOWER OF THE Flock is a famous biblical landmark with great messianic significance to both Christians and Jews.[1] In the book of Micah, the Tower of the Flock is said to be located near the Holy City.[2] This is corroborated in the Mishnah where this tower is identified with the outskirts of Jerusalem.[3] In the book of Genesis, the Tower of the Flock is located somewhere southwest of Jerusalem near the Road of the Patriarchs.[4] Tradition also places the Tower of the Flock southwest of Jerusalem but curiously situates it three miles east of the Road of the Patriarchs near Bethlehem, which does not comport well with Scripture and the Mishnah.[5] In light of the above, it may be assumed that the historical Tower of the Flock was likely located in southwest Jerusalem along the Road of the Patriarchs roughly halfway between the Shoulder of Hinnom and Bethlehem. If this is accurate and if Bible Hill is Golgotha, surely the geographic proximity of this famous messianic tower to Calvary and the birthplace of Jesus would have massively reinforced

1. See Edersheim, *Times of Jesus*, 186.
2. See Mic 4:8.
3. M. Sheqal. 7:4.
4. See Gen 35:21.
5. See Pixner, *Messiah*, 21.

the faith of the apostles in Jesus as the Christ, explaining (at least in part) the indefatigable, evangelical zeal of the apostles following the resurrection.

48

The Apostles Never Forget

That the earliest disciples of Jesus lived and worked on Mount Zion in Jerusalem throughout the Apostolic Age is one of the oldest, evidence-backed traditions in Christianity.[1] If this tradition is historically accurate, however, why does it seem counterintuitive? After all, access to the Temple cannot explain why the disciples would live on Mount Zion. Before the crucifixion, both Jesus and the disciples went to the Temple frequently but lived in Bethany. It was not about safety. In the years when Mount Zion would have served as headquarters for the Way, while they were in Jerusalem, at least eleven of the twelve apostles were jailed and whipped; Saint Stephen was stoned; James Zebedee was beheaded; Peter was nearly executed; Saint Matthias was possibly beheaded, James the Just was stoned; Paul was nearly beaten to death; and Simeon Cleophas was crucified.[2] Some might say Pentecost motivated the Nazarenes to stay on Mount Zion. This premise is logical but insufficient. After all, Jesus only commanded the apostles to stay in Jerusalem

1. See Pixner, "Church of the Apostles," 17–35.

2. See Acts 5:17–40, 5:54–60, 12:1–7, 21:31–32; Jacquier, "St. Matthias," para. 2; Josephus, *Antiquities* 20.200; and Eusebius, *Ecclesiastical History*, 273–77. It is generally assumed that Simeon Cleophas was crucified in Jerusalem, though Eusebius only records that the crucifixion happened without mentioning exactly where it occurred (see Clausen, *Upper Room*, loc. 347).

until the Holy Spirit came. He never said anything about staying in Jerusalem after that. He certainly never commanded anyone to live or work on Mount Zion. Likewise, once Jerusalem was razed in 70 CE, there was nothing on Mount Zion but rubble and Roman troops.[3] Yet, as soon as it was safe for the Nazarenes to return to Jerusalem from Pella after 70 CE, they apparently went straight back to Mount Zion and stayed.[4] Why would the early Christians do this?

At this point, many scholars will point to the traditional Calvary as a primary motivator behind the Nazarenes' desire to remain on Mount Zion. This argument is weak. Following the Roman siege of Jerusalem in 70 CE, despite there being nothing but vacant lots all around the traditional Calvary, the Nazarenes returned to the Cenacle on Mount Zion to reestablish the headquarters of the Way.[5] This makes no sense whatsoever if Jesus had been resurrected near the traditional Calvary. After all, the resurrection of Jesus is the foundation of the entire Christian religion, not the Lord's Supper or the coming of the Holy Spirit at Pentecost.[6]

The question remains then: Why would the early Christians stay on Mount Zion? First of all, if Bible Hill is Calvary, it means a platoon of soldiers from the X Roman Legion was likely on the Shoulder of Hinnom when the Nazarenes returned to Jerusalem from Pella, preventing them from settling there even if they wanted to.[7] What's more, it should be noted that the Nazarenes could have conveniently beheld the sites of the resurrection (Bible Hill), the ascension (Mount Olivet), the Last Supper (Mount Zion), and Pentecost (Mount Zion) all from the Cenacle. The Abbey of Dormition is illustrative in this regard. Early tradition identifies

3. See C. Wilson, *Holy Sepulchre*, 51–52.

4. Clausen, *Upper Room*, loc. 274. "Nazarene" is another name for the earliest Christians (see Acts 24:5). The Nazarenes lived in the city of Pella during the Roman siege of Jerusalem in 70 CE and apparently returned to Mount Zion when the war ended (ca. 74 CE).

5. See C. Wilson, *Holy Sepulchre*, 51–52.

6. See 1 Cor 15:12–19.

7. See Barkay, *Ketef Hinnom*, 15.

the site of today's Dormition Abbey on Mount Zion as the place where Lady Mary lived out her golden years in Jerusalem.[8] The site has been venerated since at least the late Roman period, and, in the early fifth century, a basilica was built there called Holy Zion. It was considered the "mother of all churches" and included the Cenacle where Lady Mary is said to have departed this life.[9] If these sacred traditions about Mary are accurate and if Bible Hill is Calvary, then logic suggests the mother of Jesus spent her final years in the Cenacle so she could gaze daily at the most sacred sites of her beloved son's glory.

8. See Watson, "Sites of Sion," 212; Adamnan, *Arculfus*, 20; and Flader, "Mary's Assumption," para. 12.

9. See Pixner, *Messiah*, 252.

49

The Politics of Goliath's Skull

One of the ultimate unanswered questions of Christianity is the mystery of why the Evangelists never explain the theological significance of the name Golgotha. They simply state as a matter of historical fact that Jesus was crucified at the place called Golgotha. While no one has come close to solving this mystery to date, if Golgotha refers to the skull of Goliath, perhaps the brevity of the Evangelists is the result of insightful prudence. In 50 CE, the first Council of Jerusalem reaffirmed the equality of Jews and gentiles in Christ Jesus, and declared that circumcision was not necessary for gentile converts.[1] Meanwhile, ultranationalist religious zealotry was on the rise in Palestine among the Jews.[2] Therefore, the Evangelists may have made a rational choice to focus only on the redemptive role of Jesus at Golgotha, not on the political connotations connected with King David, the "uncircumcised" Goliath, and the Monument of the Skull. It would have countered everything Jesus stood for if the Gospels had inadvertently triggered an ultranationalist violent insurrection in the name of Jesus of Nazareth. The fact is, Jewish zealots would have in all likelihood been both enraged and emboldened by Christ's crucifixion and

1. See Acts 15:5–21.

2. Rhoads, *Israel in Revolution*, 2.

resurrection at the Monument of (Goliath's) Skull if the Gospels had been written with even the slightest xenophobic bent. The War Scroll of Qumran and the First Jewish-Roman War are proof that such was the case in the first century when the Gospels were being composed.[3] Indeed, this threat to the gospel could partly explain why Jesus himself refused to give the apostles a straight answer when they asked him if he would immediately restore David's kingdom to Israel in Acts 1:6–8. What's more, according to tradition, sometime between 81 and 96 CE, two of Jesus' grand-nephews, Zoker and James, were arrested and interrogated by the Roman emperor Domitian for being descendants of King David.[4] Around the same time, Jesus' cousin Simeon Cleophas was crucified for being a descendent of King David.[5] Both these incidents would have reaffirmed the wisdom of the Evangelists to leave aside the political subtext of Goliath's skull in the Gospels.[6] This would also explain why no traditions connecting Goliath's skull with Calvary got passed down to later generations of Christians. Besides, the earliest followers of the Way believed that nothing stays hidden if God wants it revealed.[7] So, even if the Evangelists obscured the origins of Calvary intentionally to prevent war from breaking out in Jesus' name, they would have known the deeper truths of Golgotha would inevitably come to light if it was God's will.

3. See Aslan, *Zealot*, 58–70; Brandon, *Jesus and the Zealots*, 65; Rhoads, *Israel in Revolution*, 94; Yadin, *Scroll of the War*, 18–35. It is also telling that Josephus (writing in the late first century) obscures the fate of Goliath's skull, and alters the biblical account of David cutting off Philistine "foreskins" to say David cut off Philistine heads instead. So, it appears even the great Josephus knew better than to write about the political aspects of Goliath's skull in those volatile times.

4. See Bauckham, "Relatives of Jesus," 21.

5. See Bauckham, "Relatives of Jesus," 20; and Wenham, "Relatives of Jesus," 8.

6. See Eusebius, *Ecclesiastical History*, 273–77.

7. See 1 Cor 2:10–16.

50

The Torah Ark

In the opinion of some scholars, the Cenacle on Mount Zion contains a Judeo-Christian Torah ark from the Apostolic Age.[1] These scholars also contend that, because this alleged Torah ark faces north instead of east toward the Temple, the Nazarenes in the Cenacle must have been venerating the traditional Calvary from Mount Zion. The idea that the Cenacle contains a Torah ark does not have scholarly consensus, however, with many experts adamantly opposing the hypothesis on archaeological grounds.[2] Nor does it accord with the Madaba map, which depicts the Cenacle facing east alongside the Basilica of Holy Zion. Even if the alleged Torah ark could be proven to be from the Apostolic Age, however, its orientation is actually eleven degrees east of the traditional Calvary, pointing in the direction of Mount Hermon.[3] This is relevant because some scholars suggest Mount Hermon is the historical Mount of Transfiguration.[4] In that light, logic suggests, if the supposed Torah ark in the Cenacle is a real Torah ark dating to the time of the apostles, then it would have been built

1. See Kramer, *God Came Down*, 134–46; and Pixner, *Messiah*, 329.

2. See Murphy-O'Connor, *Holy Land*, loc. 117; Skarsaune, *Shadow of the Temple*, 189; and Joan Taylor, *Holy Places*, 215.

3. See Germano, "Ancient Church," 12–13.

4. See Sybrowsky, "Mount of Transfiguration," 64.

to venerate the mountain where Jesus was transfigured, not the traditional Calvary. This premise is bolstered by the fact that the Mount of Transfiguration is mentioned with reverence multiple times in Scripture, while nothing in northwest Jerusalem is cited anywhere in the New Testament.[5]

5. See 2 Pet 1:18 for one of the most famous references to the Mount of Transfiguration.

51

The Barsabas Tomb

Only three people are known to have been called "Barsabas" in antiquity. Two of them are related to the Nazarenes on Mount Zion.[1] The third is a man whose ossuary was excavated 1.5 miles south of Bible Hill.[2] Since only three people in antiquity are known to have been called Barsabas, logic suggests the two men named Barsabas in the New Testament were likely related to the Barsabas who was entombed near Bible Hill. It is also noteworthy that an ossuary belonging to a man named "Matthias" was also found in the same tomb where the Barsabas ossuary was discovered. This is relevant because, in the book of Acts, a Barsabas and a Matthias appear together, apparently in the Cenacle on Mount Zion.[3] What's more, this Matthias becomes one of the twelve apostles and, according to one tradition, dies by beheading in Jerusalem.[4] This is significant because the Barsabas tomb was sealed for the last time either during or just after the reign of King Herod Agrippa (r. 41–44 CE).[5] If Bible Hill is the Place of Beheading, then per-

1. See Acts 1:23, 15:22; and Pixner, "Church of the Apostles," 17–35.
2. See Sukenik, "Earliest Records of Christianity," 352.
3. See Acts 1:23; and Pixner, "Church of the Apostles," 17–35.
4. See Jacquier, "St. Matthias," para. 2.
5. See Sukenik, "Earliest Records of Christianity," 365.

haps Matthias was decapitated at Bible Hill before 44 CE, and later buried in his family tomb down the road. This would explain why Matthias disappeared so quickly from the historical record. At any rate, the Barsabas tomb remains one of the earliest archaeological discoveries ever correlated with Judeo-Christianity, and its location on the Road of the Patriarchs near Cave 34 and the Cenacle (where Barsabas and Matthias apparently appear together in the book of Acts) offers compelling geographical evidence supporting the premise that Bible Hill is the Place of Beheading. This in turn bolsters the contention that Bible Hill is Golgotha.

52

The Hill of God, Rachel's Tomb, and Calvary

According to Scripture, both the Hill of God and Rachel's tomb are located several miles north of Bethlehem, on the border of Benjamin and Judah, by the Road of the Patriarchs, close to the Tower of the Flock, near a town called Ramah, by a place called Zelzah in Benjamin, near terebinth trees, and near the former site of a Philistine boundary marker from the time of King Saul.[1] Given that Bible Hill is located several miles north of Bethlehem, on the border of Benjamin and Judah, by the Road of the Patriarchs, close to the historical site of the Tower of the Flock, near the Pilgrim of Piacenza's Ramah, near Zelzah in Benjamin (which is Jerusalem in the Talmud), near terebinth trees, and where the Hill of God would be relative to both Rachel's tomb and the Philistine boundary marker according to Scripture, logic suggests Bible Hill is both the Hill of God and near the original site of Rachel's tomb.[2]

1. See Gen 35:16–21, 48:7; Jer 31:15; Matt 2:18; 1 Sam 10:2–5; and Demsky, "Rachel," para. 30.

2. See Birch, "Nameless City," 131; Conder, "Nameless," 171; and Schwarz, *Descriptive Geography*, 109–12. As a side note, the famous terebinth tree called the Terebinth of Mary was located just south of Bible Hill near Conder's Arimathea for centuries. According to legend, Lady Mary rested under this tree while she and Joseph were on their way to Bethlehem. The Terebinth of Mary

To bolster this conclusion, consider the following additional evidence. According to Josephus, King Saul walked to the Hill of God and Rachel's tomb from a town called Aramatha, which sounds almost identical to Arimathea.[3] This suggests Conder's Arimathea could be the town where King Saul stayed before walking to the Hill of God and Rachel's tomb.[4] This assertion is sustained by the Anonymous Spanish Franciscan (on pilgrimage ca. 1550 CE) who said King Saul walked to the Hill of God and Rachel's tomb from a town just north of Bethlehem.[5] It is also plausible that the Philistines had a boundary marker near Bible Hill in the time of King Saul because the Philistines were advancing into the central hill country of Judah during his reign.[6] All this is relevant to Bible Hill as Golgotha because, to reward Abraham for his faith on Mount Moriah, Scripture says God would one day provide a "sacrificial lamb" on the "Mountain of God."[7] Since Bible Hill is

was burned down by a Saracen in 1645 to stop pilgrims from coming onto his property (see Pixner, *Messiah*, 47–48).

3. Josephus, *Antiquities* 6.47.

4. It appears no one lived on the summits of the two hills at Conder's Arimathea until the eighth century BCE, arguably because they were revered as cultic sites before then (see Lipschits et al., *Ramat Rahel IV*, 12). This makes sense if Conder's Arimathea is the settlement where Saul met Samuel before walking to Rachel's tomb. After all, Scripture says it was at the "high place" of this settlement that Samuel sacrificed animals to God, indicating it was a cultic site (see 1 Sam 9:12). Moreover, in antiquity, Conder's Arimathea was also famous for its sweet water (see Pixner, *Messiah*, 47–48). This is salient because the settlement where Saul stayed before walking to Rachel's tomb had a well or cistern. It is also important to note that the settlement where Saul stayed before walking to Rachel's tomb could have been very small (see Gen 19:20 and 1 Sam 9:6 in both the Masoretic Text and the Septuagint). This could explain why no traces of habitation from the time of King Saul remain at Conder's Arimathea. It is also noteworthy that Samuel had relatives in Bethlehem, which provides context for him being at Conder's Arimathea when Saul met him (see "Ephrathite" in 1 Sam 1:1).

5. Anonymous Spanish Franciscan, "Rome to Jerusalem," 77.

6. As to the Philistine boundary marker, while the word *netsib* is often translated as "garrison" in 1 Sam 10:5, it can also be translated as "pillar" or "boundary marker" as well. See Conder, "Pillar or Garrison?," 30.

7. See Gen 22:8–14.

called a "mountain" in the book of Joshua, it follows that (if Bible Hill is the Hill of God), it would technically be the "Mountain of God" as well—where almighty Jehovah could provide the "sacrificial lamb" as foretold in Genesis. This inference undergirds the contention that Bible Hill is Calvary because it reflects one of the subtle ways by which the geography of Golgotha may have reinforced the certainty that Jesus is the Lamb of God in the minds of early Christians.

As a side note, according to the Genesis Apocryphon (ca. 100 BCE), the valley where Abraham met Melchizedek, and where Melchizedek shared "bread and wine" with Abraham, is called the "Valley of the Vineyard House." Moreover, this valley apparently extends from Bible Hill to Bethlehem.[8] If this is correct (and if Bible Hill is both Calvary and the Hill of God), it may be assumed that the early Christians would have interpreted Bethlehem (bread), the Valley of the Vineyard House (wine), and the Hill of God (altar) as constituting some sort of supernatural, eucharistic landscape prefigured by Melchizedek's meeting with Abraham on the Shoulder of Hinnom. This would in turn explain (at least in part) how the Lord's Supper came to be one of the most important sacraments in Christianity as early as the 50s CE. Indeed, according to Scripture, the first Eucharist celebrated after the resurrection occurred at Emmaus. In that light, if Artas is Emmaus, it certainly would bolster the contention that the apostles would have viewed Bethlehem (bread), the Valley of the Vineyard House (wine), and Bible Hill (altar) as some sort of supernatural, eucharistic geography.[9]

8. See Milik, "Saint Thomas," 81–84; and Newman, "Hippodrome," 221.

9. A century ago, the area around the northern slope of Bible Hill was called Har Ariah, which means "Lion Hill" in Hebrew (Dunlop, *Faith Rewarded*, 61). Since Jesus is called the "Lion of Judah" in Scripture, this old toponym for the northern slope of Bible Hill could be evidence for Bible Hill as Golgotha. According to the Gospel of Thomas (ca. 150 CE), anyone *who eats the Lion* is blessed (Gos. Thom. 7:1). If this is alluding to Jesus as the Lion of Judah in the Eucharist (and if Lion Hill is Calvary), then suddenly another layer appears in the mystical, eucharistic landscape of Bible Hill. In that light, it is relevant to point out here that, in 1 Cor 10:18–21, the apostle Paul says the Eucharist takes place on the "table of the Lord" (*trapeza kyriou*). This phrase *trapeza kyriou* is a

53

The Counting Station of Calvary

According to the Gospel of Luke, during the reign of Herod the Great, Caesar Augustus ordered everyone in the Roman Empire to register for a census.[1] Since Bible Hill guarded all the southwestern approaches to Jerusalem and sat "outside the camp" where even the ritually defiled could be registered, it follows that, in the time of Jesus, King Herod might have established a temporary counting station by the Shoulder of Hinnom to implement Caesar's census.[2] This is relevant to Bible Hill as Golgotha because, in the Old Testament, counting stations are described as places where officials register every *golgotha* like a "head count."[3] In that light (if Bible Hill is Calvary), perhaps the census of Caesar Augustus reinforced the

---

technical term meaning the "altar of God" in the Septuagint (see Mal 1:7–12). Therefore, Paul's "table of the Lord" could have been interpreted by the early Christians as an altar representing the mystical altar on the Shoulder of Hinnom where Jesus died for the sins of mankind. (As a side note, if Bible Hill is both the Hill of God and Calvary, then it is intriguing that King Saul met "three men" carrying "bread and wine" at Golgotha [see 1 Sam 10:3–4]).

1. See Luke 2:1–5.

2. The phrase "outside the camp" is a technical phrase from the Pentateuch that refers to the time when the Jews lived in a camp after fleeing Egypt. See, for instance, Num 19:3. However, the Old Testament phrase "outside the camp" had evolved to mean "outside Jerusalem" by the first century CE.

3. See Martin, *Secrets*, 101; and Joan Taylor, "Golgotha," para. 3.

tradition of Bible Hill being called Golgotha in the time of Jesus. Indeed, in the noncanonical Gospel of James, while making her way to Bethlehem to register for the census of Caesar Augustus, Lady Mary had a prophetic vision on the Road of the Patriarchs at Conder's Arimathea in which she saw one person crying and another person celebrating.[4] According to the esteemed biblical scholar Dr. Lily Vuong, this vision of Mary's was an allusion to the death and resurrection of Jesus at Golgotha.[5] This is noteworthy because, as stated earlier, Bible Hill is just two miles from Conder's Arimathea. This indicates the Gospel of James could plausibly reflect early Judeo-Christian traditions tying the historical location of Calvary to the Road of the Patriarchs in southwest Jerusalem. This in turn bolsters the premise that Bible Hill could have been a temporary counting station where *golgothas* were being registered as Mary made her way to Bethlehem. (As a side note, about 3.5 miles south of Bible Hill today, *golgothas* are still being registered every day at Checkpoint 300 for entry into Bethlehem like a counting station would have operated at Bible Hill for the census of Caesar Augustus.)[6]

4. See Shoemaker, *Mary*, 1–8. As one of the earliest pieces of Christian literature outside the New Testament, the Gospel of James (ca. 150 CE) can be cautiously used to investigate Scripture and reinforce biblical archaeology.

5. See Vuong, *James*, 9.

6. See Rijke, "Checkpoint," 337.

The View of Mount Zion from the Proposed Counting Station of Calvary at Bible Hill[7]

7. "Mt. Zion," photo by American Colony (Jerusalem), ca. 1900–1920. Matson photograph collection, U.S. Library of Congress, used with permission.

54

Gabbatha and More Crucifixions

A Roman governor by the name of Florus ordered a salvo of crucifixions (around 65 CE) from his judgment seat on Gabbatha.[1] The key to connecting this salvo of death to Bible Hill is the location where Florus crucified his victims. Josephus says the crucifixions took place outside King Herod's palace in front of the tribunal. Since Bible Hill sits before Gabbatha and since crucifying people on Bible Hill would have been seen by almost everyone in Jerusalem, logic suggests Florus crucified his victims on Bible Hill, thus bolstering the assertion that Bible Hill is Golgotha. It is notable, however, that a crucifixion nail was excavated in the ruins of Gabbatha.[2] In view of this, perhaps a literal reading of Josephus is in order, and Florus really did crucify his victims right before Gabbatha next to the Judgment Gate. It is also conceivable that Florus crucified his victims in a mad frenzy of sickening brutality from the Judgment Gate all the way to Bible Hill. Either way, the crucifixions did not take place at the traditional Calvary, Gordon's Calvary, or the miphkad altar.

1. See Josephus, *War* 2.301–308.
2. See Tabor, "Face of Jesus," 33:08–41.

55

General Titus

In 70 CE, during the Roman siege of Jerusalem, General Titus ordered his soldiers to crucify any Jews caught fleeing the Holy City.[1] As a result, at least five hundred Jews a day were nailed to crosses in full view of the city walls.[2] When General Titus ordered these mass crucifixions, the Roman army was pressing Jerusalem from the north via the tomb of John Hyrcanus and the Antonia Fortress. This indicates many of the Jews fleeing the city would have been caught on the Shoulder of Hinnom and crucified on Bible Hill.[3] This is relevant to Bible Hill as Golgotha because it demonstrates once again how the geography of Bible Hill renders it the perfect place for crucifying people in accordance with the savage standards of antiquity. (As a side note, perhaps the coin excavated in Cave 34 from the later Bar Kokhba Revolt came from someone crucified by the Romans on Bible Hill in the course of that conflict.)[4]

1. See Josephus, *War* 5.449.
2. See Josephus, *War* 5.450–451.
3. See Vieweger et al., "DEI," 275.
4. See Kloner and Zissu, *Necropolis*, 362.

A Column of Soldiers in the Hinnom Valley Where General Titus Besieged the Praetorium in 70 CE[5]

5. "Palestine Disturbances: The Scots Guard Parade Preceded by the Band," photo by American Colony (Jerusalem), 1936. Matson photograph collection, U.S. Library of Congress, used with permission.

56

The Northwest Battlefield

THE TRADITIONAL CALVARY SITS in the middle of a major battlefield from the Roman siege of Jerusalem in 70 CE.[1] This is critical to mention because, if Jesus had really been crucified at the traditional Calvary, then Josephus would have surely mentioned this at least once in his narration of the fighting that took place there. After all, Josephus knew perfectly well who Jesus was.[2] Indeed, in one section of *Antiquities*, he even devotes an entire paragraph to Jesus. Josephus also grew up in Jerusalem at the height of the Apostolic Age when the Nazarenes were extremely active converting thousands of Jews to the Way.[3] It is inconceivable therefore that Josephus did not know the location of Jesus' crucifixion. It is worth noting that, despite not mentioning Jesus (or Calvary) in relation to this battlefield, Josephus does mention the tomb of John Hyrcanus multiple times and locates it in the immediate vicinity of the traditional Calvary.[4] To be certain, as the esteemed archaeologist Fr. Thomas Reilly states in the *Catholic Encyclopedia*, "[the traditional Calvary is] located in the district . . . described by Josephus

1. See Josephus, *War* 5.248–289, 5.296–361, 5.466–472, 6.169–176.
2. See Schmidt, *Josephus and Jesus*, 198–214.
3. See Acts 2:41.
4. See Josephus, *War* 5.259, 5.304, 5.356, 5.468, 6.169.

as containing the monument of the high priest John."[5] It is also noteworthy that, despite Gordon's Calvary being close to the place where the Romans likely breached the Second Wall in the battle for northern Jerusalem, neither Jesus nor Calvary was mentioned by Josephus in connection with this place either. All this naturally favors Bible Hill as Golgotha.

The Northwest Battlefield[6]

5. Reilly, "Mount Calvary," para. 3.

6. "The Pool of Hezekiah, Jerusalem," photo by Francis Frith, ca. 1862. U.S. Library of Congress, used with permission.

57

The Tomb of John Hyrcanus

At this point, critics of Bible Hill as Golgotha could highlight the fact that Josephus never pinpoints the exact location of the tomb of John Hyrcanus. The Hyrcanus tomb could have been twenty or more yards away from the traditional Calvary for all anyone knows. This is true. However, evidence such as pollen samples, ancient ashlars, and road-network analysis indicates the tomb of John Hyrcanus was located on the exact site of the traditional Calvary in the time of Jesus. Recently, for instance, pollen samples from grapevines and olive trees were discovered under the Church of the Holy Sepulcher at first-century levels.[1] This suggests cultivated gardens such as the ones that adorned King Herod's mausoleum at the Herodium could have surrounded the tomb of John Hyrcanus there in the time of Jesus.[2] Several limestone ashlars near the traditional Calvary under the Church of the Redeemer also appear to date to the Herodian Dynasty.[3] If this is correct, it means these ashlars could have originally come from the tomb of John Hyrcanus at the traditional site of Calvary. This prospect is plausible because King Herod highly esteemed John

1. See Windle, "Ancient Garden," para. 1.
2. See Netzer, *Palaces*, 132.
3. See Gibson and Taylor, *Beneath the Church*, 18.

Hyrcanus and would have built a funerary monument for him at the traditional site of Calvary as a result.[4] Moreover, according to Fr. Charles Couasnon and Dr. Dan Bahat, the rock outcropping called the Rock of Calvary in the Church of the Holy Sepulcher could have formerly been part of a grand funerary monument (such as the tomb of John Hyrcanus).[5] This assertion by Fr. Couasnon and Dr. Bahat is also bolstered by the testimony of Cyril of Jerusalem (dating ca. 348 CE), who states that a portico (that could have adorned the tomb of John Hyrcanus) decorated the original entrance of the traditional tomb of Christ before Queen Helena and Bishop Macarius tore it down.[6] In addition, during archaeological excavations, a finely hewn stone with an elegant chip-carved rosette was discovered under the Church of the Holy Sepulcher. This stone appears to have been part of a ceiling decoration originally, and it probably dates to the early Roman period.[7] If this is accurate, it means the stone could have come from an ornamental ceiling in the tomb of John Hyrcanus. What's more, the asymmetrical orientation of the present Greek Patriarchate Street in relation to Aelia's forum is evidence that, in the time of Jesus, this same street could have led to a northwest entrance to the tomb of John Hyrcanus.[8] The best piece of evidence for the tomb of John Hyrcanus having been located at the Church of the Holy Sepulcher, however, is the present-day Christian Quarter Road. According to research by the distinguished archaeologist Dr. Dominique-Marie Cabaret, in 70 CE, the Roman general Titus attacked the Upper City of Jerusalem via today's Christian Quarter Road, which happens to dead-end by the Church of the Holy Sepulcher.[9] If Dr. Cabaret is correct about Titus's battle plan, then logic strongly suggests the Roman general utilized the present site of the Church of the Holy Sepulcher as a

4. See Tabor, *Lost Mary*, 73–74.

5. See Couasnon, *Schweich Lectures*, 39–40; and Bahat, "Burial," 32.

6. See Duckworth, *Church of the Holy Sepulchre*, 89–90; and Gibson and Taylor, *Beneath the Church*, 61.

7. Gibson and Taylor, *Beneath the Church*, 17.

8. See Cabaret, *Topography*, 282–84.

9. Cabaret, *Topography*, 14–17.

fortified position from which to launch his assault on the Upper City. This undergirds the premise that the traditional Calvary is the tomb of John Hyrcanus because Josephus makes it clear that Titus planned to attack and capture the Upper City by way of the sepulcher of the high priest John.[10]

The Likely Site of the Tomb of John Hyrcanus[11]

10. Josephus, *War* 5.259, 5.356.

11. "Façade du St. Sépulchre," photo by Maison Bonfils, ca. 1867–1899. U.S. Library of Congress, used with permission.

58

The Gentile Christians Forget

In 132 CE, the Jews launched a massive insurrection across Palestine in the name of the messiah Simon bar Kokhba. The insurrection lasted three years, which enraged the Romans. When Rome finally triumphed over the Jewish rebels in 135 CE, Emperor Hadrian was so infuriated, he evicted every Jew in Jerusalem and ordered that no Jew be allowed to enter the Holy City ever again. Furthermore, if any Jew was caught trying to enter Jerusalem in violation of this ban, he would be summarily put to death. Moreover, "except, possibly, during the later years of the reign of Septimius Severus (A.D. 193–211), the order forbidding Jews to approach the city was strictly enforced, and there was no relaxation until the reign of Emperor Constantine."[1] As a result, starting in 135 CE, "political necessity dictated the election of a Gentile bishop [in Jerusalem] . . . [and the Christian] Church fell more and more under the influence of Greek thought and sentiment."[2] The division between Christianity and Judaism "soon became complete, and the Church eventually branded as heretics those Judeo-Christians, such as the Nazarenes or Ebionites, who held to the law and rejected Paul as

1. C. Wilson, *Holy Sepulchre*, 68. See Avi-Yonah *Byzantine Rule*, 79–81; and Joan Taylor, *Holy Places*, 48–51.

2. C. Wilson, *Holy Sepulchre*, 68. See Turner, "Episcopal Lists," 553.

an exponent of Christianity. So great was the revulsion in feeling, that the place upon which the Temple of Jehovah had stood was, in course of time, regarded as accursed and profane."[3] To be sure, according to the infamous first-century Christian bishop Marcion, Jehovah was not even God.[4] Meanwhile, also in 135 CE, the Romans started rebuilding Jerusalem in their own image, calling it "Aelia Capitolina" in honor of the emperor Hadrian.[5] Soon the city was thoroughly transformed, destroying virtually every point of reference that might have been used in later centuries to locate first-century holy sites. Indeed, the changes to the city were so extensive, even the precise location of the Second Temple remains uncertain to this day.[6]

With virtually no landmarks left from the first century for orientation and no Judeo-Christians around to guide them, it appears Queen Helena and Bishop Macarius resorted to torture to extract the information they needed to locate Calvary.[7] Certainly, in 400 CE, the Roman historian Sozomen reported that Macarius consulted a Jew from the diaspora to find Golgotha. Later, Gregory of Tours identified this Jew as one "Judas of the East." Then, in 700 CE, Emperor Leo of Byzantium revealed that, in Helena's search for the true cross, the Queen tortured as many Jews as she could find around Jerusalem to extract the location of Golgotha. When this failed to elicit the desired information, she threw one Jew in particular into a cistern to suffer there until he divulged the location of the true cross.[8] Eventually, on the verge of death, this Jew showed Helena where the true cross could be found. If Emperor Leo's account is accurate, then these three stories taken together indicate a Jew from the East named Judas was tortured by Helena and Macarius until he divulged the location of the traditional

3. See Kim, "Emperor Leo III," 251; and C. Wilson, *Holy Sepulchre*, 68.

4. See Conybeare, *Origins of Christianity*, 329.

5. See Weksler-Bdolah, *Aelia Capitolina*, 51.

6. See Martin, *Jerusalem Forgot*, 110–11.

7. See Birch, "Golgotha on Mount Zion," 140–41; and Kim, "Emperor Leo III," 251.

8. See C. Wilson, *Holy Sepulchre*, 89.

Calvary.[9] If this was the case, it would explain (at least in part) why Helena and Macarius searched for Calvary in the area where the tomb of John Hyrcanus had once stood. As one of the most famous Jewish leaders in history, John Hyrcanus would have been known to this Judas of the East. Moreover, the location of the Hyrcanus tomb would have been easy for Judas to identify because a pagan temple of Venus would have been sitting on top of it since the reign of the emperor Hadrian.[10] What's more, studies show that, to escape the pain of torture, even the most scrupulous of people will provide interrogators with false, unreliable, or misleading information.[11] It would have been natural, therefore, for this Judas of the East to have misled Helena and Macarius to escape the torture chamber.

It should be mentioned that, in the opinion of some scholars, the tradition of Helena torturing Jews to find Calvary is pure legend.[12] These scholars assert that Helena would not have been present in Jerusalem in 326 CE to torture anyone because she would have been too old and too important to have taken the arduous sea journey to arrive in Palestine in time to commit such an atrocity. They also highlight the fact that Eusebius only credits Constantine and Macarius with finding the traditional Calvary, a fact which apparently undercuts the premise that Helena was in Palestine to torture Jews to locate Golgotha. However, it could just as easily be argued that Helena's advanced age and her importance are the very reasons why she would have taken such an improbable sea journey to arrive in Palestine by the end of 326 CE. At nearly eighty years of age, Helena could have died on any given day, and she would have known this. It stands to reason therefore that she would have been highly motivated to reach the Holy Land as soon as possible, and she would have possessed all the economic and political clout needed to achieve this goal. As to Eusebius only giving credit to

9. See Birch, "Golgotha on Mount Zion," 140–41.

10. See Tabor, *Lost Mary*, 73; Joan Taylor, *Holy Places*, 113–42; and C. Wilson, *Holy Sepulchre*, 100.

11. See Einolf, "Torture Fails," para. 1.

12. See Hillner, *Helena Augusta*, 208–46.

Constantine and Macarius for the finding of the traditional Calvary, let it be remembered that the discovery of the traditional site of Golgotha was anything but normal. It represented the ultimate triumph of Christianity over paganism. Against this background, it makes sense that Eusebius would have erased Helena's role in the search for Calvary to make sure she could never outshine her son in this epic chapter of Roman history. In this way, Eusebius would have been maximizing the chances of Christianity becoming the preeminent religion throughout the male-dominated Roman Empire. Indeed, as a veteran of the game of thrones, perhaps Helena herself ordered Eusebius not to give her credit. This would explain why Eusebius never mentions Helena vis-à-vis the discovery of the traditional Calvary while so many subsequent ancient chroniclers do (e.g., Ambrose, Monachus, Rufinus, Socrates, Sozomen, Theodoret, and Theophanes, to name but a few).

59

Inside the Walls of Aelia

If the location of Golgotha was truly unknown in the fourth century, why did Queen Helena and Bishop Macarius look for it inside the walls of Aelia? After all, Scripture clearly states that Jesus was crucified and buried outside Jerusalem, not inside the city. In that light, logic suggests there is no way Helena and Macarius would have looked for Calvary under the Temple of Venus within the walls of Aelia unless they were extremely confident in the authenticity of the traditional site. This inference must be accounted for if Bible Hill is to be taken seriously as a credible site for Golgotha. It so happens a plausible answer to this question lies with the venerable St. Jerome and the Jewish historian Josephus. According to Jerome, in the fourth century, there were multiple sites outside Jerusalem called Calvary.[1] What's more, it is clear from the historical record that no one knew which of these Calvaries was the historical Golgotha, (explaining why Helena and Macarius had to look for it). It may be assumed therefore that, in the search for the biblical Calvary, both Helena and Macarius would have realized (based on a reading of Josephus) that the tomb of John Hyrcanus had been outside the walls of first-century Jerusalem in the area where Hadrian built his Temple of Venus. This

1. See C. Wilson, *Holy Sepulchre*, 21–22.

would have reinforced the credibility of Judas's confession that the tomb of Christ had been buried under the Temple of Venus, thereby explaining the confidence Helena and Macarius placed in the traditional Calvary. Plus, by locating Jesus' tomb under the Temple of Venus, Helena and Macarius could justify the demolition of what they must have considered to be a pagan monstrosity in the heart of Aelia. Building the Church of the Holy Sepulcher within the walls of Aelia would have been prudent as well, as it would have protected the luxurious basilica from attacking armies and marauders outside the city.

As a side note, once the traditional Calvary got the stamp of approval by Constantine, the Christians in Aelia quickly concluded that Emperor Hadrian buried the tomb of Christ under the city's Temple of Venus on purpose to obliterate the memory of Jesus.[2] This slander probably arose from a combination of befogged tales of Hadrian burying the tomb of John Hyrcanus and shock that no one in Aelia had ever heard of the tomb of Christ being under the Temple of Venus before Queen Helena and Bishop Macarius told them.

2. See C. Wilson, *Holy Sepulchre*, 193.

60

The Exception of the Cenacle

If the location of Calvary was forgotten after the Bar Kokhba Revolt, how could the less important site of the Cenacle be preserved well into the fourth century? This question must be accounted for because much of the evidence underpinning Bible Hill as Golgotha depends on the authenticity of the Cenacle. It so happens a plausible answer to this question lies with Jesus' cousin Simeon Cleophas and the X Roman Legion.

In the wake of the Roman siege of Jerusalem in 70 CE, tradition suggests the Cenacle on Mount Zion was rebuilt by Simeon Cleophas about 150 yards south of the X Legion camp.[1] This is plausible because Simeon's uncle Joseph and cousin Jesus were both skilled builders, so it is possible Simeon was one too.[2] If this is correct, then it may be assumed that, following the reconstruction of the Cenacle, successive groups of legionnaires would have converted to Christianity after 70 CE and worshiped with the Nazarenes on Mount Zion accordingly.[3] This is not baseless speculation either. "The fact that Christian soldiers served in the Roman legions in the centuries before Constantine is demonstrable from

1. See Pixner, *Messiah*, 332–33.
2. See Tabor, "Carpenter," para. 3.
3. See Clausen, *Upper Room*, loc. 3029–37.

both literary and archaeological evidence."[4] The Roman centurion Cornelius in the book of Acts is a case in point.

Then came the Bar Kokhba Revolt. Given the destructive nature of war, it is likely that the Cenacle was damaged during the rebellion, but the large, Herodian ashlars that made up its foundation preserved its location.[5] It would be logical to assume therefore that, following the revolt, the returning Christian soldiers rebuilt the Cenacle on its original site, calling it the "Church of the Apostles" (because it was located on the spot where the apostles ate the Last Supper and received the Holy Spirit at Pentecost). The strength of this assumption is buttressed by the fact that Judas Kyriakos, who was the last Judeo-Christian bishop of Jerusalem, would have likely aided the soldiers in this endeavor.[6] What's more, despite the Nazarenes being banished from Jerusalem after 135 CE, logic suggests the legacy of Pentecost would have prompted successive groups of X Legion Christians to lay claim to the Cenacle as their exclusive place of worship.[7]

When the X Legion left Aelia (and Bible Hill) around 300 CE, the Cenacle was apparently neglected for eighty years.[8] This was arguably on account of orthodox Christians such as Eusebius and Macarius viewing the Cenacle and its former X Legion occupants with suspicion and disdain due to their heretical "Judeo-Christian" leanings. Indeed, according to Hippolytus (as preserved in his *Apostolic Tradition*, ca. 215 CE), Christians in the legions were so heretical, he called for their excommunication.[9] If all this is accurate, it would certainly explain why, when Helena visited Jerusalem, Macarius never took her to Mount Zion.[10] Only years later, when the Holy Spirit was proclaimed by the church to be the

4. Clausen, *Upper Room*, loc. 2992.
5. See Pixner, *Messiah*, 333.
6. See Rousseau and Arav, *Jesus and His World*, 117.
7. See Bieberstein, "Hagia Sion," 545.
8. See Pixner, *Messiah*, 341.
9. See Clausen, *Upper Room*, loc. 3008.
10. See Clausen, *Upper Room*, loc. 568.

Third Person of the Trinity, did the orthodox Christians embrace the Cenacle as their own.[11]

As a side note, with the endemic chaos inflicting the Roman Empire during the Crisis of the Third Century, it may be assumed that the invasion and five-year occupation of Jerusalem by Queen Zenobia (269–74 CE) caused the already beclouded memory of Bible Hill as Calvary to become irreversibly befogged in the litany of opinions regarding which place of beheading in Jerusalem was the actual Golgotha of Scripture.[12] At the same time, even if the Christian legionnaires had competing opinions about the location of the Church of the Apostles when they reoccupied Aelia in 274, the unmistakable Herodian ashlars that made up the Cenacle's foundation would have once again settled the debate.[13]

The Traditional Site of the Cenacle on Mount Zion[14]

11. See Bieberstein, "Hagia Sion," 546.

12. See Andrade, *Zenobia*, 165–215; and Clausen, *Upper Room*, loc. 453.

13. See Clausen, *Upper Room*, loc. 2559–77. The large ashlars in the foundation of the Cenacle would have also been highly resistant to earthquakes.

14. "Tomb of David and Cenacle, Jerusalem," photo by Felix Bonfils, ca. 1870. In Bonfils, *Souvenirs d'Orient*.

61

The Saracens of Mount Zion

After the Muslims conquered Palestine in 636 CE, evidence indicates some of the remaining Judeo-Christians in Israel returned to Jerusalem.[1] Moreover, in the opinion of the esteemed biblical scholar Dr. David Flusser, while the Muslims ruled the Holy Land, pockets of stalwart Judeo-Christians managed to survive in the shadows until at least the tenth century.[2] If Dr. Flusser is correct about the Judeo-Christians holding out for so long, it makes Fr. Felix Fabri's account of the Saracens who rejected the Church of the Holy Sepulcher all the more fascinating to report.[3] According to Fr. Fabri (on pilgrimage ca. 1483 CE), certain Saracens and Eastern Christians practiced superstitious observances beneath a fig tree near the Cenacle where there was also a great heap of stones.[4] To this spot, Saracen women came every day to burn incense and bury loaves of bread (like some kind of eucharistic ritual) because they asserted the tomb of Jesus was near the Cenacle on Mount Zion, not in northwest Jerusalem at the Church

1. See Pixner, *Messiah*, 378.
2. Flusser, *Jewish Sources*, 82.
3. See Fabri, *Wanderings*, 332.
4. See C. Wilson, *Holy Sepulchre*, 106–7.

of the Holy Sepulcher.[5] Fr. Fabri also said these Saracen women baptized their children and prayed to Jesus. In view of the above, perhaps these women were not Saracens at all, but were in fact secret Judeo-Christians inconspicuously preserving highly beclouded versions of the original traditions of the Nazarenes in southwest Jerusalem, thus boosting the odds that Bible Hill is Golgotha.

5. See Fabri, *Wanderings*, 332.

62

Bishop Melito

THAT BISHOP MELITO (100–180 CE) was a highly respected, prolific Christian theologian is a recognized fact.[1] This pedigree is one of the reasons why some scholars consider Melito's homily called *Peri Pascha* (written after Melito's trip to Jerusalem in 160 CE) as reliable evidence for the authenticity of the traditional Calvary.[2] In *Peri Pascha*, Melito says Jesus was crucified in the middle of Jerusalem.[3] If this statement by Melito is taken literally, it means Melito must have believed the location of the historical Calvary was in the middle of second-century Jerusalem where the Church of the Holy Sepulcher would be built by Constantine in the fourth century. This apparently supports the premise that Helena and Macarius did not blindly or deceptively choose the traditional site of Golgotha but based their decision on traditions handed down to them from the second century or earlier.

A literal interpretation of Melito's location for Calvary becomes highly problematic, however, in view of the myriad contradictions and factual errors contained in *Peri Pascha*.[4] In one verse,

1. See MacErlean, "Melito of Sardis," para. 1.

2. See Harvey, "Melito and Jerusalem," 401–40; and Joan Taylor, "Golgotha," para. 19.

3. See Stewart-Sykes, *On Pascha*, 56.

4. See Nautin, "Homelie de Meliton," 429.

for instance, Melito says Jesus was crucified during the day. Yet, in another verse, he says Jesus was crucified at night. Then, in a third verse, he says Jesus could not have been crucified at night. Taken together, these three verses are totally illogical and contradictory. Then, elsewhere in the homily, Melito says Jesus was entombed after sunset, completely violating Scripture. The fact is, according to all four Gospels, Jesus was buried before sundown, not at night. Accordingly, "it becomes evident that the chronological and geographical details of Melito's Peri Pascha cannot be used as a basis for determining . . . the location of Golgotha."[5]

Since "Aelia" was the official name of Jerusalem when Melito wrote *Peri Pascha*, it stands to reason that, if the bishop had really been referring to the actual location of Calvary in his homily, he would have said Jesus was crucified in the middle of "Aelia," not in the middle of Jerusalem. To be certain, writing in 330 CE, in the years when Christianity was already being actively championed by Emperor Constantine, Eusebius nevertheless states in his famous list of biblical locations that "Golgotha . . . is indeed pointed out in Aelia."[6] Similarly, writing in 388 CE, Jerome states, "Golgotha—the Place of Calvary . . . [which] is pointed out in Aelia."[7] Seeing as both Eusebius and Jerome called Jerusalem "Aelia" in their descriptions of the location of Calvary in their day, then surely Melito would have done the same in his if his intent in *Peri Pascha* had likewise been to relate the literal location of Calvary to his parishioners.

Also consider Melito's admiration of the emperor Hadrian. According to Paulinus of Nola (writing ca. 396 CE), Hadrian built a temple of Venus over Calvary following the Bar Kokhba Revolt to obliterate the memory of Jesus.[8] This is notable because, nine years after his pilgrimage to Jerusalem, Bishop Melito wrote a letter in which he praised Hadrian.[9] This makes no sense if Hadrian built a pagan temple over Calvary in the middle of Jerusalem to

5. Von Wahlde, "Time and Place," 569.
6. Quoted in Joan Taylor, *Onomasticon*, 45.
7. Quoted in Joan Taylor, *Onomasticon*, 45.
8. See C. Wilson, *Holy Sepulchre*, 64–65.
9. See Grant, "Marcus Aurelius," 7.

obliterate the memory of Jesus. It would, however, make perfect sense if Hadrian built a temple of Venus over the tomb of John Hyrcanus.[10] In simple terms, if Hadrian buried the tomb of John Hyrcanus following the Bar Kokhba Revolt instead of the tomb of Christ, it would explain how Bishop Melito could still praise Emperor Hadrian in good conscience following his pilgrimage to Jerusalem.[11] It follows, therefore, that, in writing *Peri Pascha*, Bishop Melito said Jesus died in the middle of Jerusalem for no other reason than to extol the sacrifice of Jesus in a highly dramatic way, not provide his parishioners with directions to the tomb of Christ under the Temple of Venus in second-century Aelia Capitolina.

As a side note, in Rome, eight memorial panels from a monument dedicated to Hadrian were prominently displayed on Constantine's victory arch celebrating Constantine's triumph over Maxentius on the Milvian Bridge.[12] Since Constantine attributed this victory to the power of Christ, it stands to reason, if Hadrian had built a temple of Venus over Calvary to obliterate the memory of Jesus, there is no way Constantine would have decorated his arch with these memorial panels honoring Hadrian.[13] It is also notable that, according to the Roman historian Cassius Dio (writing ca. 229 CE), the Sepulcher of Solomon still stood in Jerusalem during the Bar Kokhba Revolt. It stands to reason therefore that the tomb of John Hyrcanus could have still been standing (for Hadrian to later bury) at the outbreak of the Bar Kokhba Revolt as well.

10. See Martin, *Secrets*, 260.

11. See Stewart-Sykes, *On Pascha*, 57.

12. See Opper, *Hadrian*, 173.

13. See Leithart, *Defending Constantine*, 68–71. These panels have all been altered to make Hadrian look like Constantine. Nevertheless, it remains extremely unlikely that Constantine would have ever used them in the first place if Hadrian had buried the tomb of Christ to obliterate the memory of Jesus.

63

The Geography of Eusebius

ACCORDING TO EUSEBIUS, GOLGOTHA was located "right beside (*pros*) the northern parts (*tois boreiois*) of Mount Zion."[1] Advocates of the traditional site of Golgotha frequently use this statement by Eusebius to bolster the validity of the traditional Calvary because certain evidence shows Eusebius made this statement before Queen Helena and Bishop Macarius launched their search for Calvary in 326 CE.[2] However, other evidence indicates Eusebius made this statement sometime between 326 and 330 CE after the traditional Calvary had been identified by Helena and Macarius.[3] In this light, it is possible that Eusebius said Golgotha was north of Mount Zion because he was parroting what Queen Helena and Bishop Macarius were already saying themselves. To do otherwise would have been playing with fire as well. After all, it is a documented fact that when Helena arrived in Jerusalem to

1. Joan Taylor, "Golgotha," para. 23.

2. Joan Taylor, *Onomasticon*, 3.

3. See H. Chadwick, *Ancient Society*, 718; Duchesne, *Early History*, 130; McClintock and Strong, "Paulinus" para. 1; and Wallace-Hadrill, *Eusebius of Caesarea*, 56–57. The key to determining when Eusebius said Calvary was located north of Mount Zion is knowing the year in which Paulinus of Tyre got promoted to the bishopric of Antioch, which occurred sometime between 323 and 330 CE (see H. Chadwick, *Ancient Society*, 718).

meet Macarius, her beloved son Constantine had recently murdered one of her grandsons, and Helena herself may have played a role in the murder of Constantine's wife.[4] The fact is, both Helena and Constantine were ruthless autocrats who would crush anyone who got in their way.[5] Eusebius would have known this all too well and would have protected himself accordingly when writing about the location of Calvary.[6] (Incidentally, this would also plausibly explain why Eusebius documented no events postdating the year 324 in his multivolume history of the Christian church. By leaving out current events, such as the discovery of the traditional Calvary, in his history, Eusebius may have been ensuring that nothing in his book could inadvertently cause it to be banned or lead to his own persecution by the imperial family.) Lastly, even if it could somehow be proven that Eusebius said Calvary was north of Mount Zion before 326 CE, his location for Golgotha could still be totally wrong. To be sure, in his famous *Onomasticon*, Eusebius makes one of the greatest gaffes in the history of biblical geography when he locates the tomb of King David in Bethlehem instead of Jerusalem.[7] It is conceivable therefore that he might have made a similar blunder with the location of Calvary.

4. See Hillner, *Helena Augusta*, 178–203; and Woods, "Empress Fausta," 70–79.

5. See Potter, *Constantine the Emperor*, 161–93.

6. See Duckworth, *Church of the Holy Sepulchre*, 87.

7. Joan Taylor, *Onomasticon*, 31.

64

The Ship Graffito

In 1971, the sketch of a ship and its corresponding inscription were found on the surface of a smooth-faced stone embedded in one of the many ancient foundation walls under the Church of the Holy Sepulcher. Today, proponents of the traditional site of Golgotha often present this ship and its inscription as evidence that Christian pilgrims were worshiping Jesus at Hadrian's Temple of Venus in Aelia before Bishop Macarius and Queen Helena certified the historicity of the traditional Calvary, thus bolstering its authenticity.[1] This narrative is highly misleading, however. Indeed, according to the esteemed biblical scholars Dr. Shimon Gibson and Dr. Joan Taylor, the boat and its inscription could date to the first century.[2] This means (for all anyone knows) the ship and its inscription could have been sketched on the side of a pagan shrine by heathen legionnaires when Hadrian was still a child (and later repurposed to build Aelia's Temple of Venus). Plus, no scholarly consensus even exists on what the inscription actually says. What's more, it appears the ship drawing was significantly altered in the 1970s. At some point between 1971 and 1975, "there [were] alterations which . . . resulted in the transformation of the Jerusalem

1. See, for instance, Flattery, "Lord, We Have Come," paras. 5–7.
2. Gibson and Taylor, *Beneath the Church*, 48.

ship drawing . . . . The present drawing is but a poor reflection of the unique ship representation that existed in 1971. Many [original] details of the ship have now been lost."[3] In light of the above, there can be no certainty in the premise that a Christian pilgrim drew this ship or wrote its inscription.

How does this enhance the prospect of Bible Hill being Golgotha, however? It enhances it because it demonstrates again that nothing connects the crucifixion of Jesus to the site of the traditional Calvary before the time of Queen Helena and Bishop Macarius. This means the only evidence from antiquity underpinning the authenticity of the Church of the Holy Sepulcher are dreams, visions, and perhaps the confession of a Jew under torture.[4] Compare that to the straightforward logic of Jesus being crucified in front of the Praetorium on the Road of the Patriarchs up high on a hill that looks like a giant skullcap.

As a side note, to explain the lack of Christian graffiti at Bible Hill, one must consider that, over the last two thousand years, the Judeans, Romans, Syrians, Byzantines, Persians, Umayyads, Abbasids, Crusaders, Ayyubids, Mamluks, Turks, Brits, Jordanians, and Israelis have all damaged or altered the northern slope of Bible Hill in one way or another. Even the Iron Age tombs on Bible Hill have been used and reused so many times by so many different people over the last two millennia that whatever Christian graffiti may have existed in them at one time has been obliterated. A relatively recent event in the long history of Bible Hill (during the late Ottoman period) is a case in point: One of the Iron Age burial caves on Bible Hill "was reused by the Turkish army . . . as an arms and ammunition depot, probably for troops stationed in the nearby [Fort Gazelle]. An explosion destroyed the roof of the burial cave [along with any evidence of Christian graffiti on it]."[5]

3. Gibson and Taylor, *Beneath the Church*, 34.

4. See C. Wilson, *Holy Sepulchre*, 80–92.

5. Barkay, "Riches of Ketef Hinnom," 25.

65

The Church of St. George Outside the Walls

As early as the fourth century, the Romans built an exquisite basilical church on the northern slope of Bible Hill.[1] This church was truly regal, with handsome ashlars, ornate mosaics, and colored glass tesserae that decorated the walls of the church. It was large as well, being fifty yards in length and almost thirty yards in width.[2] The church had a crypt, large cisterns, and auxiliary buildings for baking wafers used in the Eucharist. In the opinion of Dr. Gabriel Barkay, this church was the "Church of St. George Outside the Walls" that was mentioned by Thomas the Undertaker in 808 CE in his book on the churches of Jerusalem.[3]

If this church was the Church of St. George Outside the Walls, then logic suggests its patron saint was St. George because Christian cavalrymen of the Roman-Moorish Equestrian Regiment were executed on Bible Hill between 303 and 311 CE as a result of

1. See Bar-Am and Bar-Am, "Where the Ancients," para. 4; and Barkay, "Riches of Ketef Hinnom," 25–26.

2. See Barkay, *Ketef Hinnom*, 13.

3. See Avner and Zelinger, "Cemetery," 141; and Barkay, "Riches of Ketef Hinnom," 26. An inscription near the Shoulder of Hinnom supports the identification of this church as the Church of St. George Outside the Walls. Numismatic evidence, however, does not substantiate this identification. For this reason, the identification of this church as the Church of St. George Outside the Walls must remain tentative.

the anti-Christian purges of Emperor Diocletian.[4] This is conceivable because St. George was a Roman soldier who was executed just thirty miles west of Bible Hill in 303 CE because of his faith in Jesus.[5] What's more, evidence shows the execution of St. George immediately effected a cult of personality, turning George into a prodigious military saint across the Christian world.[6] It follows then that the fame of St. George would have been great around Jerusalem when Emperor Constantine decriminalized Christianity ten years after St. George's death. Indeed, in the fourth century, especially following Constantine's reforms, "martyred Christian soldiers . . . were routinely honored and celebrated by the laity."[7] It stands to reason then that the memory of Christian cavalrymen being executed on Bible Hill would have lingered in the minds of Jerusalem's Christians. As a result, in the decades following the Edict of Milan, the Christians of Jerusalem would have been highly motivated to build an exquisite basilical church on Bible Hill to honor these unjustly executed soldiers of Christ.

The fate of this magnificent church is shrouded in mystery. According to Thomas the Undertaker, in 614 CE the Persians slaughtered the priests who worked in the Church of St. George Outside the Walls.[8] This means (if the church on Bible Hill is the Church of St. George Outside the Walls and if Bible Hill is Golgotha) this massacre of the priests in 614 CE constitutes the last recorded case of executions at Calvary. At some point in the early Ottoman period "the church was badly damaged . . . when many building-stones were removed, perhaps for the construction of the nearby [Fort Gazelle]."[9]

4. See Bieberstein, "Aelia Capitolina," 159.
5. See Thurston, "St. George," para 1.
6. See Thurston, "St. George," para 2.
7. Quoted in Clausen, *Upper Room*, loc. 3009.
8. See Barkay, *Ketef Hinnom*, 13.
9. Barkay, *Ketef Hinnom*, 13.

The Suggested Site of the Church of St. George Outside the Walls[10]

10. "St. Andrews Church, Jerusalem. St. Andrew's Church Showing 'Y' bldg. [i.e., Building], K.D. [i.e., King David] Hotel & Citadel," photo by American Colony (Jerusalem), ca. 1934–39. Matson photograph collection, U.S. Library of Congress, used with permission.

66

Conclusion

THE EVIDENCE NOW INDICATES Bible Hill is the historical location of Golgotha. Jeremiah 31:39 and Gen 3:15 are obvious sources of scriptural inspiration for a crucifixion on Bible Hill. The former is connected to the new covenant that Jesus proclaimed in the Cenacle and fulfilled at Golgotha. The latter is the fulfillment of God's prophecy that Christ would crush the head of the Enemy, symbolized by the skull of Goliath under the cross of David at Bible Hill. (See Ezek 34:23 for the name of David signifying Christ.) It would also be sensible to cite 1 Cor 1:18 and Isa 53:5 as scriptural inspiration for a crucifixion on Bible Hill. This is because the "foolishness of the cross" implies Jesus was "pierced for our transgressions" somewhere utterly baffling like the Monument of the Skull. The forensic evidence favoring Bible Hill as Calvary, however, is what really puts Bible Hill in a class of its own. For the first time in two thousand years, it is now possible to follow Jesus from the Cenacle, to Gethsemane, to Caiaphas's mansion, to the Praetorium, and finally to Calvary based on rational geography, archaeology, literary evidence, and logical inference. This constitutes a total revolution in biblical geography, and it signifies the resurrection of the historical Calvary.

Bibliography

Abel, Felix-Marie. "Petites Decouvertes au Quartier du Cenacle à Jerusalem." *Revue Biblique (1892–1940)* 8 (1911) 119–25.

Adamnan. *The Pilgrimage of Arculfus in the Holy Land.* Translated by James Rose MacPherson. London: Palestine Pilgrims' Text Society, 1889.

Adler, Rivkah. "The Way of the Patriarchs: You Have to Know the Bible to Win." *Jerusalem Post,* Mar. 12, 2022. https://www.jpost.com/christianworld/article-701095.

Allison, Dale. *The New Moses: A Matthean Typology.* Eugene, OR: Wipf & Stock, 1993.

Amit, David, and Shimon Gibson. "Water to Jerusalem: The Route and Date of the Upper and Lower Level Aqueducts." In *Cura Aquarum in Israel II: Water in Antiquity, Proceedings of the 15th International Conference of the History of Water Management and Hydraulic Engineering in the Mediterranean Region, Israel, 14–20 October 2012,* edited by Christoph Ohlig and Tsvika Tsuk, 9–42. Siegburg: Schriften der Deutschen Wasserhistorischen Gesellschaft, 2014.

Andrade, Nathanael. *Zenobia: Shooting Star of Palmyra.* New York: Oxford University Press, 2018.

Anonymous Spanish Franciscan. "Narrative of a Journey from Rome to Jerusalem." Translated by H. L. Pink and H. C. Luke. *Palestine Exploration Fund Quarterly Statement* 57 (June/Oct. 1925) 140–50, 193–206.

———. "Narrative of a Journey from Rome to Jerusalem." Translated by H. L. Pink and H. C. Luke. *Palestine Exploration Fund Quarterly Statement* 58 (Jan./Apr./July/Oct. 1926) 23–28, 74–82, 136–43, 196–206.

Aslan, Reza. *Zealot: The Life and Times of Jesus of Nazareth.* New York: Random House, 2013.

Avigad, Nahman. *The Herodian Quarter in Jerusalem: Wohl Archaeological Museum.* Jerusalem: Keter, 1991.

Avi-Yonah, Michael. *The Jews Under Roman and Byzantine Rule: A Political History from the Bar Kokhba War to the Arab Conquest.* New York: Magnes, 1976.

———. "The Third and Second Walls of Jerusalem." *Israel Exploration Journal* 18 (1968) 98–125.

Avner, Rina, and Yehiel Zelinger. "A Cemetery, a Quarry, and Remains of a Church at Ketef Hinnom, Jerusalem." *Atiqot* 80 (2015) 23–53 [Heb.], 141–42 [Eng.].

———. "Jerusalem, Ketef Hinnom." *Hadashot Arkheologiyot: Excavations and Surveys in Israel* 113 (2001) 82–84.

Bacher, Wilhelm, and Jacob Lauterback. "Sanhedrin." *The Jewish Encyclopedia*, 1906. https://www.jewishencyclopedia.com/articles/13178-sanhedrin.

Bagatti, Bellarmino C. *The Church from the Circumcision: History and Archaeology of the Judeo-Christians*. Translated by Eugene Hoade. Jerusalem: Franciscan, 1971.

Bahat, Dan. "Does the Holy Sepulchre Church Mark the Burial of Jesus?" *Biblical Archaeology Review* 12 (May/June 1986) 26–45.

Baldensperger, Philip J. "The Immovable East (Continued)." *Palestine Exploration Fund Quarterly Statement* 36 (Jan. 1904) 128–37.

Bar-Am, Aviva. "Exploring Former No-Man's Land: A Desolate Expanse Has Been Transformed into Stunning Parks and Unique Promenades." *Jerusalem Post*, Jan. 15, 2015. https://www.jpost.com/in-jerusalem/exploring-former-no-mans-land-387849.

Bar-Am Aviva, and Shmuel Bar-Am. "The Kibbutz Outside Jerusalem Built Atop an Ancient Palace." *The Times of Israel*, Sept. 17, 2016. https://www.timesofisrael.com/the-kibbutz-outside-jerusalem-built-atop-an-ancient-palace/.

———. "Where the Ancients Left Their Dead: A Walk Through History in Downtown Jerusalem." *The Times of Israel*, May 11, 2019. https://www.timesofisrael.com/where-the-ancients-left-their-dead-a-walk-through-history-in-downtown-jerusalem/.

Barclay, James T. *The City of the Great King: Jerusalem as It Was and as It Was Meant to Be*. Philadelphia: J. B. Lippincott, 1858.

Barkay, Gabriel. "Excavations on the Slope of the Hinnom Valley, Jerusalem." *Oadmoniot: A Journal for the Antiquities of Eretz-Israel and Bible Lands* 4 (1984) 94–108.

———. "The Garden Tomb: Was Jesus Buried Here?" *Biblical Archaeology Review* 12 (1986) 40–57.

———. *Ketef Hinnom: A Treasure Facing Jerusalem's Walls*. Jerusalem: The Israel Museum, 1986.

———. "Mounds of Mystery: Where the Kings of Judah Were Lamented." *Biblical Archaeology Review* 29 (May/June 2003) 32–39, 66, 68.

———. "The Riches of Ketef Hinnom: Jerusalem Tomb Yields Biblical Text Four Centuries Older Than Dead Sea Scrolls." *Biblical Archaeology Review* 35 (July/Oct. 2009) 22–35, 122–24.

———. "Royal Palace, Royal Portrait? The Tantalizing Possibilities of Ramat Rahel." *Biblical Archaeology Review* 32 (2006) 34–44.

Bibliography

Barkay, Gabriel, et al. "A Late Iron Age Fortress North of Jerusalem." *Bulletin of the American Schools of Oriental Research* 328 (Nov. 2002) 49–71.

Bartlett, William H. *Walks About the City and Environs of Jerusalem.* 2nd ed. London: Virtue Brothers, 1846.

Bauckham, Richard. "The Relatives of Jesus." *Themelios* 21 (Jan. 1996) 18–21.

Baumgarten, Albert I. "Josephus on Essene Sacrifice." *Journal of Jewish Studies* 45 (Autumn 1994) 169–83.

Beekes, Robert. *Etymological Dictionary of Greek.* Vol. 1. Boston: Brill, 2010.

Bell, Rob. *Love Wins: A Book About Heaven, Hell, and the Fate of Every Person Who Ever Lived.* New York: Harper One, 2011.

Ben-Daniel, John. "The Essenes and Jerusalem." *Qumran Chronicle* 30 (Dec. 2022) 77–118.

———. *The Essenes of Mount Arbel and Jerusalem: Origins, History, and Influence.* Krakow: Enigma, 2023.

Berdai, M. Adnane, et al. "Postobstructive Pulmonary Edema Following Accidental Near-Hanging." *American Journal of Case Reports* 14 (Sept. 2013) 350–53.

Bernard the Wise. *The Itinerary of Bernard the Wise.* Translated by J. H. Bernard. London: Palestine Pilgrims' Text Society, 1893.

Beswick, Samuel. "The Place Called Bethso." *Palestine Exploration Fund Quarterly Statement* 12 (Apr. 1880) 108–9.

Betz, Otto. "Was John the Baptist an Essene?" *Biblical Archaeology Review* 6 (Dec. 1990) 18–25.

Bieberstein, Klaus. "Aelia Capitolina." In *Jerusalem Before Islam, BAR International Series 1699*, edited by Zeidan Kafafi, and Robert Schick, 134–68. Oxford: Archeopress. 2007.

———. "Die Hagia Sion in Jerusalem: Zur Entwicklung ihrer Traditionen im Spiegel der Pilgerberichte." In *Akten des Xii. Internationalen Kongresses fur Christliche Archaologie, Bonn 1991*, edited by Ernst Dassmann and Josef Engemann, 543–51. Munster: Aschendorffsche Verlagsbuchhandlung, 1995.

Billig, Yaakov. "The Upper Aqueduct to Jerusalem, the Church of the Kathisma, and Other Remains near Hebron Road." *Antiqot* 69 (2012) 69–90.

Birch, William F. "The City of David and Josephus." *Palestine Exploration Fund Quarterly Statement* 16 (Jan. 1884) 77–82.

———. "Golgotha on Mount Zion." *Palestine Exploration Fund Quarterly Statement* 39 (Jan. 1907) 140–47.

———. "The Nameless City." *Palestine Exploration Fund Quarterly Statement* 11 (July 1879) 130–31.

———. "Zion, the City of David." *Palestine Exploration Fund Quarterly Statement* 10 (Oct. 1878) 178–89.

Bishop, Mike C. *Handbook to Roman Legionary Fortresses.* South Yorkshire: Pen and Sword, 2012.

Blenkinsopp, Joseph. "Kiriath-Jearim and the Ark." *Journal of Biblical Literature* 88 (1969) 143–56.

Bliss, Frederick J. *Excavations at Jerusalem, 1894–1897*. London: Committee of the Palestine Exploration Fund, 1898.

———. "Third Report on the Excavations at Jerusalem." *Palestine Exploration Fund Quarterly Statement* 27 (Jan. 1895) 9–25.

Bohstrom, Philippe. "Archaeologists Uncover Life of Luxury in 2,000-Year-Old Priestly Quarters of Jerusalem." *Haaretz*, July 12, 2016. https://www.haaretz.com/archaeology/2016-07-12/ty-article/priestly-quarter-of-ancient-jerusalem-found-on-mt-zion/.

Bolen, Todd. "Nose Falls Off the Skull of Gordon's Calvary." *BiblePlaces Blog*, Mar. 2, 2015. https://www.bibleplaces.com/blog/2015/03/nose-falls-off-skull-of-gordons-calvary/.

Bond, Helen K. *Caiaphas: Friend of Rome and Judge of Jesus?* London: Westminster/John Knox, 2004.

———. *The Historical Jesus: A Guide for the Perplexed*. New York: Bloomsbury, 2012.

Bonfils, Felix. *Souvenirs d'Orient: Album Pittoresque des Sites, Villes, et Ruines les Plus Remarquables de la Terre-Sainte*. A Alais (Gard): Chez L'auteur, 1878.

Brandon, Samuel. *Jesus and the Zealots*. New York: Scribner's, 1967.

Brodrick, Mary. *The Trial and Crucifixion of Jesus Christ of Nazareth*. New York: Longmans Green, 1908.

Broshi, Magen. "Along Jerusalem's Walls." *Biblical Archaeologist* 40 (1977) 11–17.

———. "Excavations in the House of Caiaphas, Mount Zion." In *Jerusalem Revealed: Archaeology in the Holy City, 1968–1974*, edited by Yadin Yigael, 57–60. Jerusalem: Israel Exploration Society, 1975.

———. "Excavations on Mount Zion, 1971–1972: Preliminary Report." *Israel Exploration Journal* 26 (1976) 81–88.

Buchard of Mount Zion. *A Description of the Holy Land*. Translated by Aubrey Stewart. London: Palestine Pilgrims' Text Society, 1896.

Cabaret, Dominique-Marie. *The Topography of Ancient Jerusalem, 2nd Century BC—2nd Century AD: Essays on the Urban Planning Record, Defences, and Gates*. Translated by David Orton. Series Archaeologica of the Cahiers de la Revue Biblique 4. Paris: Peeters, 2022.

Cary, Otis, and Frank Cary. "How Old Were Christ's Disciples?" *Biblical World* 50 (July 1917) 3–12.

Caspari, Christian E. *A Chronological and Geographical Introduction to the Life of Christ*. Translated by Maurice Evans. Edinburgh: T & T Clark, 1876.

Cassels, Walter. *The Gospel According to Peter: A Study*. London: Longmans Green, 1894.

Chadwick, Henry. *The Church in Ancient Society: From Galilee to Gregory the Great*. New York: Clarendon, 2001.

Chadwick, Jeffrey R. "Revisiting Golgotha and the Garden Tomb." *Religious Educator: Perspectives on the Restored Gospel* 4 (2003) 13–48.

Charlesworth, James. *The Beloved Disciple: Whose Witness Validates the Gospel of John?* Valley Forge, PA: Trinity Press International, 1995.

Chrysostom, John. *Discourses Against Judaizing Christians.* Translated by Paul W. Harkins. The Fathers of the Church 68. Washington, DC: The Catholic University of America Press, 1979.

Cioffi-Revilla, Claudio. "Origins and Age of Deterrence: Comparative Research on Old World and New World Systems." *Cross-Cultural Research* 33 (1999) 239–64.

Claeys, J., et al. "Magical Practices? A Non-Normative Roman Imperial Cremation at Sagalassos." *Antiquity* 97 (2023) 158–75.

Clausen, David C. *The Upper Room and Tomb of David: The History, Art, and Archaeology of the Cenacle on Mount Zion.* Kindle. Jefferson, NC: McFarland, 2016.

Clermont-Ganneau, Charles. "The So-Called Tomb of Joseph of Arimathea." In *The Survey of Western Palestine: Jerusalem*, edited by Charles Warren and Claude Conder, 319–27. London: Committee for the Palestine Exploration Fund, 1884.

Colon, Peter. "Gordon's Calvary." *Israel My Glory*, May/June 2023. https://israelmyglory.org/article/gordons-calvary/.

Conder, Claude. *The City of Jerusalem.* London: John Murray, 1909.

———. "Emmaus." In *A Dictionary of the Bible Dealing with Its Literature and Contents Including the Biblical Theology*, edited by James Hastings, 1:700. Edinburgh: T. & T. Clark, 1889.

———. "The Holy Sepulchre." *Palestine Exploration Fund Quarterly Statement* 15 (Apr. 1883) 69–78.

———. "The Nameless City." *Palestine Exploration Fund Quarterly Statement* 11 (Oct. 1879) 171–72.

———. *Palestine.* London: George Philip & Son, 1889.

———. "Pillar or Garrison?" *Palestine Exploration Fund Quarterly Statement* 16 (Jan. 1884) 30.

———. "The Rock Scarp of Zion." *Palestine Exploration Fund Quarterly Statement* 7 (Apr. 1875) 81–89.

———. "The Survey of Palestine: Letters from Lieut. Claude R. Conder, R. E." *Palestine Exploration Fund Quarterly Statement* 4 (Oct. 1872) 153–73.

———. "The Zion Scarp." *Palestine Exploration Fund Quarterly Statement* 7 (Jan. 1875) 7–10.

Conder, Francis, and Claude Conder. *A Handbook to the Bible: Being a Guide to the Study of the Holy Scriptures.* London: Longmans Green, 1879.

Conybeare, Fred C. *The Origins of Christianity.* New York: University Books, 1958.

Cornuke, Robert. *Golgotha: Searching for the True Location of Christ's Crucifixion.* Coeur d'Alene, ID: Koinonia, 2016.

Couasnon, Charles. *The Church of the Holy Sepulcher in Jerusalem: The Schweich Lectures, 1972.* London: British Academy, 1974.

Crawford, Deborah. "St. Joseph and Britain: The Old French Origins." *Arthuriana* 11 (2001) 1–20.

Crawley-Boevey, Arthur W. "Golgotha and the Holy Sepulchre." *Palestine Exploration Fund Quarterly Statement* 38 (Oct. 1906) 269–74.

———. "Map and Description of Jerusalem by Christian Van Adrichem (1533–1585)." *Palestine Exploration Fund Quarterly Statement* 41 (Jan. 1909) 64–68.

———. "Recent Opinions on the Site of Calvary." *Palestine Exploration Fund Quarterly Statement* 42 (Jan. 1910) 23–26.

Crossan, John Dominic. *Jesus: A Revolutionary Biography*. New York: HarperCollins, 2009.

———. *Who Killed Jesus? Exploring the Roots of Anti-Semitism in the Gospel Story of the Death of Jesus*. San Francisco: Harper, 1995.

Culpepper, R. Alan. *John the Son of Zebedee: The Life of a Legend*. Columbia: University of South Carolina Press, 1994.

Cutler, Allan. "Does the Simeon of Luke 2 Refer to Simeon the Son of Hillel?" *Journal of Bible and Religion* 34 (1966) 29–35.

Dalman, Gustaf. *Sacred Sites and Ways: Studies in the Topography of the Gospels*. Translated by Paul Levertoff. New York: Macmillan, 1934.

Daniel. *The Pilgrimage of the Russian Abbot Daniel in the Holy Land (1106–1107)*. Annotated by Charles W. Wilson. London: Palestine Pilgrims' Text Society, 1888.

Daniel, C. "Les 'Herodiens' du Nouveau Testament sont-ils des Esseniens?" *Revue de Qumran* 6 (1967) 53.

David, Ariel. "Archaeologists Find the Last Hideout of the Jewish Revolt in Jerusalem." *Haaretz*, May 10, 2016. https://www.haaretz.com/archaeology/2016-05-10/ty-article/.premium/archaeologists-find-jewish-rebels-last-hideout/.

———. "Are These Nails from Jesus' Crucifixion? New Evidence Emerges, but Experts Are Unconvinced." *Haaretz*, Oct. 12, 2020. https://www.haaretz.com/archaeology/2020-10-12/ty-article/jerusalem-nails-jesus-christ-crucifixion-romans-caiaphas-tomb/.

Demandt, Alexander. *Pontius Pilate*. Munich: Beck, 2012.

Deming, David. "The Aqueducts and Water Supply of Ancient Jerusalem." *Ground Water* 63 (July/Aug. 2025) 649–60.

Demsky, Aaron. "Where Was Rachel Buried?" *TheTorah.com*, 2023. https://www.thetorah.com/article/where-was-rachel-buried.

Donaldson, G. H. "Signaling Communications and the Roman Imperial Army." *Britannia* 19 (1988) 349–56.

Donnelly, D. E., and P. J. Morrison. "Hereditary Gigantism—The Biblical Giant Goliath and His Brothers." *Ulster Medical Journal* 83 (May 2014) 86–88.

Drijvers, Jan Willem. "The True Cross: Separating Myth from History." *Bible Review* 19 (Aug. 2003) 24–33.

Driscoll, James F. "Nicodemus." *The Catholic Encyclopedia*, 1911. http://www.newadvent.org/cathen/11066b.htm.

Duchesne, Louis. *Early History of the Christian Church: From Its Foundation to the End of the Fifth Century.* Vol. 2. 4th ed. New York: Longmans Green, 1912.

Duckworth, Henry. *The Church of the Holy Sepulchre.* New York: AMS, 1980.

Dunlop, Walter T. *Faith Rewarded: The Story of St. Andrew's Scots Memorial Church, Jerusalem.* Peterborough, Eng.: Upfront, 2014.

Edersheim, Alfred. *The Life and Times of Jesus the Messiah.* Vol. 1. New York: E. R. Herrick, 1900.

———. *The Temple, Its Ministry, and Its Services as They Were at the Time of Jesus.* Boston: IRA Bradley, 1881.

Edwards, William, et al. "On the Physical Death of Jesus Christ." *Journal of American Medical Association* 255 (1986) 1455–63.

Einolf, Christopher. "How Torture Fails: Evidence of Misinformation from Torture-Induced Confessions in Iraq." *Journal of Global Security Studies* 7 (Mar. 2022). https://doi.org/10.1093/jogss/ogab019.

Ellicott, Charles. *A New Testament Commentary for English Readers.* Vol. 1. New York: Dutton, 1879.

Erlich, Zeev H. "The Garden of Uzza in Ketef Hinnom." In *Judea and Samaria Research Studies*, edited by Yaacov Eshel, 5:61–79. Kedumim-Ariel: The Research Institute—The College of Judea and Samaria, 1995.

Eusebius. *The Ecclesiastical History.* Vol. 1. Translated by Kirsopp Lake. London: William Heinemann, 1926.

———. *The Life of the Blessed Emperor Constantine.* London: Samuel Bagster and Sons, 1845.

———. *Proof of the Gospels.* Translated by William Ferrar. Grand Rapids: Baker, 1981.

Fabri, Felix. *The Book of the Wanderings of Felix Fabri.* Translated by Aubrey Stewart. London: Palestine Pilgrims' Text Society, 1892.

Fetellus. *Fetellus (Circa 1130 A.D.).* Translated by James Rose MacPherson. London: Palestine Pilgrims' Text Society, 1896.

Finegan, Jack. *The Archaeology of the New Testament: The Life of Jesus and the Beginning of the Early Church.* Princeton, NJ: Princeton University Press, 1992.

Finn, Elizabeth A. "Emmaus Identified." *Palestine Exploration Fund Quarterly Statement* 15 (Jan. 1883) 53–64.

Flader, John. "Where Was the Place of Mary's Assumption?" *Catholic Leader*, Aug. 12, 2023. https://catholicleader.com.au/life/faith/qa-where-was-the-place-of-marys-assumption/.

Flattery, Amy. "'Lord, We Have Come'—The Pilgrim Boat." Assemblies of God, Apr. 3, 2020. https://news.ag.org/en/article-repository/news/2020/04/lord-we-have-come-the-pilgrim-boat.

Flusser, David. *Jewish Sources in Early Christianity.* Tel Aviv: Naidat, 1989.

Franz, Gordon. "More on Simcha Jacobovici and the Nails from Caiaphas' Tomb." Associates for Biblical Research, Apr. 21, 2011. https://biblearchaeology.

org/research/contemporary-issues/3091-more-on-simcha-jacobovici-and-the-nails-from-caiaphas-tomb.

Fuller, Thomas. *Bisgah Sight of Palestine and the Confines Thereof with the History of the Old and New Testament Acted Thereon*. London: William Tegg, 1869.

Furgeson, James. *An Essay on the Ancient Topography of Jerusalem*. London: John Weale, 1847.

Garsiel, Moshe. "David's Warfare Against the Philistines in the Vicinity of Jerusalem (2 Sam. 5:17–25; 1 Chron. 14:8–16)." In *Studies in Historical Geography*, edited by G. Galil and M. Weinfeld, 150–64. Vetus Testamentum Supplements 81. Leiden: Brill, 2000.

Gautier, Lucien. "Remarks on the July, 1901, 'Quarterly Statement.'" *Palestine Exploration Fund Quarterly Statement* 34 (Jan. 1902) 77–78.

Germano, Michael. "The Ancient Church of the Apostles: Revisiting Jerusalem's Cenacle and David's Tomb." *Near East Archaeology Society* 1 (2003) 1–27.

Geva, Hillel. "Jerusalem's Population in Antiquity: A Minimalist View." *Tel Aviv* 41 (2014) 131–60.

———. "The 'Tower of David'—Phasael or Hippicus?" *Israel Exploration Journal* 31 (1981) 57–65.

Gibson, Shimon. *The Cave of John the Baptist: The First Archaeological Evidence of the Historical Reality of the Gospel Story*. New York: Doubleday, 2004.

———. *The Final Days of Jesus: The Archaeological Evidence*. Kindle. New York: HarperCollins, 2009.

———. "Suggested Identifications for 'Bethso' and the 'Gate of the Essenes' in the Light of Magen Broshi's Excavations on Mt. Zion." In *New Studies in the Archaeology of Jerusalem and Its Region, Collected Papers*, edited by Joseph Patrich and David Amit, 1:25–33. Jerusalem: Israel Antiquities Authority and the Hebrew University of Jerusalem, 2007.

———. "The Trial of Jesus at the Jerusalem Praetorium." In *The World of Jesus and the Early Church*, edited by Craig A. Evans, 97–118. Peabody, MA: Hendrickson, 2011.

Gibson, Shimon, and Joan Taylor. *Beneath the Church of the Holy Sepulcher, Jerusalem*. London: Committee of the Palestine Exploration Fund, 1994.

Gill, Dan. "Appendix 1: Bedrock Geology and Building Stones in the Western Wall Plaza Excavations and the Jerusalem Area." In *The Roman and Byzantine Remains: Architecture and Stratigraphy*, by S. Weksler-Bdolah and A. Onn, 209–50. Vol. 1 of *Jerusalem Western Wall Plaza Excavations*. Jerusalem: Israel Antiquities Authority, 2019.

Glatt, Benjamin. "The Holy Sepulchre's Long History." *The Jerusalem Post*, Sept. 13, 2016. https://www.jpost.com/Christian-News/The-Holy-Sepulchres-long-history-467608.

Gonen, Rivka. *Biblical Holy Places: An Illustrated Guide*. New York: Paulist, 2000.

Goris, Harm. "Thomas Aquinas on Christ's Descent into Hell." In *The Apostles' Creed "He Descended into Hell,"* edited by Marcel Sarot and Archibald van

Wieringen, 93–114. Studies in Theology and Religion 24. Leiden: Brill, 2018.

Gourinard, Henri. "The Emmaus Trail." *Bible History Daily*, June 10, 2025. https://www.biblicalarchaeology.org/daily/biblical-sites-places/the-emmaus-trail/.

Grant, Robert. "Five Apologists and Marcus Aurelius." *Vigiliae Christianae* 42 (Mar. 1988) 1–17.

Grass, Hans. *Ostergeschehen und Osterberichte*. Gottingen: Vandenhoeck and Ruprecht, 1956.

Greenhut, Zvi. "Horbat Illit." *Hadashot Arkheologiyot—Excavations and Surveys in Israel (HA-ESI)* 119 (Nov. 6, 2007). https://doi.org/10.69704/jhaesi.116.2004.532.

Guerin, Victor. *Description Géographique, Historique, et Archéologique de la Palestine*. Vol. 1. Paris: L'Imprimerie, 1868.

Haelewyck, Jean-Claude. "The Old Syriac Versions of the Gospels: A Status Quaestionis (From 1842 to the Present Day)." *Babelao* 8 (2019) 141–79.

Hanauer, James E. "Notes on the Controversy Regarding the Site of Calvary." *Palestine Exploration Fund Quarterly Statement* 24 (Oct. 1892) 295–308.

———. "The Place of Stoning." *Palestine Exploration Fund Quarterly Statement* 13 (Oct. 1881) 317–19.

———. *Walks About Jerusalem*. London: Getty Research Institute, 1910.

Harl, Marguerite. *La Bible d'Alexandrie*. Paris: La Genese, 1986.

Harvey, A. E. "Melito and Jerusalem." *Journal of Theological Studies* 17 (1966) 401–40.

Haupt, Paul. "Golgotha." *Proceedings of the American Philosophical Society* 59 (1920) 237–44.

Helms, Svend W. "The Jerusalem Ship, ISIS MYRIONYMOS, and the True Cross." *International Journal of Nautical Archaeology and Underwater Exploration* 9 (1980) 105–20.

Herman, Danny. "Following Jesus in Jerusalem #28: The Elusive Second Wall." YouTube video, Feb. 10, 2022. https://www.youtube.com/watch?v=rRb1Mfzn-A4.

Hertzberg, Hans. *I and II Samuel: A Commentary*. Philadelphia: Westminster, 1964.

Hill, John G. "The Site of Golgotha and the Holy Sepulchre." *Palestine Exploration Fund Quarterly Statement* 34 (Jan. 1902) 93–94.

Hillner, Julia. *Helena Augusta: Mother of the Empire*. New York: Oxford University Press, 2023.

Hirsch, Emil, et al. "Elijah." *The Jewish Encyclopedia*, 1906. https://jewishencyclopedia.com/articles/5634-elijah.

Hirsch, Emil, and Schulim Ochser. "Nicodemus (Nakdimon) Ben Gorion." *The Jewish Encyclopedia*, 1906. https://jewishencyclopedia.com/articles/11526-nicodemus-nakdimon-ben-gorion.

Hirsch, Emil, and Ira Price. "Tophet." *The Jewish Encyclopedia*, 1906. https://jewishencyclopedia.com/articles/14445-tophet.

Hoffmeier, James. "David's Triumph over Goliath: 1 Samuel 17:54 and Ancient Near Eastern Analogues." In *Egypt, Canaan, and Israel: History, Imperialism, Ideology, and Literature*, edited by S. Bar et al., 87–114. Boston: Brill, 2011.

Howard, George. *Hebrew Gospel of Matthew*. Macon, GA: Mercer University Press, 1995.

Howe, Fisher. *The True Site of Calvary: Suggestions Relating to the Resurrection*. New York: Anson D. F. Randolph, 1871.

Hrimat, Heba. "The Monastery of St. Onuphrius on the Field of Blood." Eastern Orthodox Patriarchate of Jerusalem, July 2, 2021. https://en.jerusalem-patriarchate.info/articles-speeches/the-monastery-of-st-onuphrius-on-the-field-of-blood/.

Humphreys, Sarah C. "The Jerusalem Ship." *International Journal of Nautical Archaeology and Underwater Exploration* 3 (1974) 309–10.

Humphries, Colin. *The Mystery of the Last Supper*. Cambridge: Cambridge University Press, 2011.

Hutchinson, Robert F. "Further Notes on Our Lord's Tomb." *Palestine Exploration Fund Quarterly Statement* 5 (July 1873) 113–15.

———. "Notes on Our Lord's Tomb." *Palestine Exploration Fund Quarterly Statement* 2 (June/Sept. 1870) 379–81.

———. "The Tomb of Our Lord." *Palestine Exploration Fund Quarterly Statement* 25 (Jan. 1893) 79–80.

Ilmsens. "Ground Penetrating Radar: Searching for the Second Wall in Jerusalem." July 6, 2020. https://www.ilmsens.com/the-search-for-the-second-wall-in-jerusalem/.

Jacquier, Jacque E. "St. Matthias." *The Catholic Encyclopedia*, 1911. https://www.newadvent.org/cathen/10066a.htm.

Jeremias, Joachim. *Golgotha*. Leipzig: Von Eduard, 1926.

———. *Jerusalem in the Time of Jesus: An Investigation into Economic and Social Conditions During the New Testament Period*. Philadelphia: Fortress, 1969.

Jerome. *Commentary on Matthew*. Translated by T. P. Scheck. The Fathers of the Church 117. Washington, DC: The Catholic University of America Press, 2008.

John of Wurzburg. *Description of the Holy Land by John of Wurzburg*. Translated by Aubrey Stewart. London: Palestine Pilgrims' Text Society, 1890.

Jones, Arnold H. *The Herods of Judea*. Oxford: Clarendon, 1938.

Jones, Victoria. "The Unnamed Emmaus Disciple: Mary, Wife of Cleopas?" *Art and Theology* (blog), Apr. 28, 2017. https://artandtheology.org/2017/04/28/the-unnamed-emmaus-disciple-mary-wife-of-cleopas/.

Josephus. *Antiquities*. Translated by Patrick Rogers. 2010. https://www.biblical.ie/page.php?fl=josephus/Antiquities/AJE01.

———. *War of the Jews*. Translated by Patrick Rogers. 2010. https://www.biblical.ie/page.php?fl=josephus/War/WE01.

Kato-Noguchi, Hisashi, and Midori Kato. "The Invasive Mechanism and Impact of *Arundo Donax*, One of the World's 100 Worst Invasive Alien Species." *Plants* 14 (2025). https://doi.org/10.3390/plants14142175.

Keim, Theodor. *The History of Jesus of Nazara: Considered in Its Connection with the National Life of Israel and Related in Detail.* Vol. 6. Translated by Arthur Ransom. London: Williams and Norgate, 1883.

Keshman, Anastasia. "Walking in the Footsteps of Christ in Latin, Greek, or Russian: On the Various Ways of the Via Dolorosa in 19th Century Jerusalem." *Romische Historische Mitteilungen* 61 (2019) 89–116.

Kim, Seonyoung. "The Arabic Letters of the Byzantine Emperor Leo III to the Caliph Umar Ibn Abd al-Aziz: An Edition, Translation, and Commentary." PhD diss., The Catholic University of America, 2017.

King, Charles W. *The Gnostics and Their Remains.* London: David Nutt, 1887.

Kitto, John. *Modern Jerusalem.* London: Religious Tract Society, 1846.

Kloner, Amos. "Did a Rolling Stone Close Jesus' Tomb?" *Biblical Archaeology Review* 25 (Sept./Oct. 1999) 22–29, 76.

———. *Survey of Jerusalem: The Northeastern Sector.* Jerusalem: Israel Antiquities Authority, 2001.

Kloner, Amos, and Boaz Zissu. *The Necropolis of Jerusalem in the Second Temple Period.* Dudley, MA: Peeters, 2007.

Kochav, Sarah. "The Search for a Protestant Holy Sepulchre: The Garden Tomb in Nineteenth Century Jerusalem." *Journal of Ecclesiastical History* 46 (Apr. 1995) 278–301.

Kohler, Kaufmann, and Ludwig Blau. "Gehenna." *The Jewish Encyclopedia*, 1906. https://www.jewishencyclopedia.com/articles/6558-gehenna.

Kokkinos, Nikos. *The Enigma of Jesus the Galilean.* Athens: Chryse Tome, 1980.

Kosloski, Philip. "How Much Might Judas' 30 Pieces of Silver Be Worth Today?" *Aleteia*, 2017. https://aleteia.org/2017/04/12/how-much-might-judas-30-pieces-of-silver-be-worth-today.

Kosmala, Hans. *Hebraer-Essener-Christen.* Leiden: Brill, 1959.

Kraeling, Carl H. "The Episode of the Roman Standards at Jerusalem." *Harvard Theological Review* 35 (Oct. 1942) 263–89.

Krafft, Wilhelm. *Die Topographie Jerusalem.* Bonn: H. B. Konig, 1846.

Kramer, Joel. *Where God Came Down: The Archaeological Evidence.* Brigham City, UT: Expedition Bible, 2020.

Kreyenbuhl, J. "Der Ort der Verurteilung Jesu." In *Zeitschrift fur die Neutestamentliche Wissenschaft und die Kunde des Urchristentums*, edited by Erwin Preuschen, 15–22. Giessen: J. Ricker'sche Verlagsbuchhandlung, 1902.

Kubis, Adam. "Jesus' Trial Before Herod Antipas." *Resovia Sacra* 21 (2014) 239–77.

Lane, Thomas. "Jesus as High Priest: The Significance of the Seamless Robe." St. Paul Center, 2025. https://stpaulcenter.com/posts/jesus-as-high-priest-the-significance-of-the-seamless-robe.

Laney, Carl J. "The Identification of Emmaus from Selective Geographical Problems in the Life of Christ." PhD diss., Dallas Theological Seminary, 1977.

Lee, James W., and Robert Bain. *The New Testament Illustrated and Explained.* St. Louis: N. D. Thompson, 1895.

Leithart, Peter. *Defending Constantine: The Twilight of an Empire and the Dawn of Christendom.* Downers Grove, IL: IVP Academic, 2010.

Lemonon, Jean-Pierre. *Pilate et le Gouvernement de la Judee: Textes et Monuments.* Paris: Gabalda, 1981.

Le Strange, Guy. *Palestine Under the Muslims: A Description of Syria and the Holy Land from A.D. 650 to 1500.* London: Alexander P. Watt, 1890.

Lewis, Agnes S. *A Translation of the Four Gospels from the Syriac of the Sinaitic Palimpsest.* New York: Macmillan, 1894.

Liddell, Henry, and Robert Scott. *A Greek English Lexicon.* Oxford: Clarendon, 1968.

Lidz, Franz. "In a Roman Tomb, 'Dead Nails' Reveal an Occult Practice." *New York Times*, Mar. 25, 2023. https://www.nytimes.com/2023/03/25/science/archaeology-ancient-rome-tomb.html.

Lipschits, Oded, et al. *Ramat Rahel IV: The Renewed Excavations by the Tel Aviv-Heidelberg Expedition (2005–2010), Stratigraphy and Architecture.* Monograph Series 39. University Park, PA: Eisenbrauns, 2020.

Lonnqvist, Minna, and Kenneth Lonnqvist. *Archaeology of the Hidden Qumran: The New Paradigm.* Helsinki: Helsinki University Press, 2002.

Lucan. *The Civil War.* Translated by James D. Duff. London: William Heinemann, 1928.

MacErlean, Andrew. "Melito of Sardis." *The Catholic Encyclopedia*, 1911. https://www.newadvent.org/cathen/10166b.htm.

MacKenzie, Anouk. "The Plants: How to Remove Bay Area Weeds." In *The Weed Workers' Handbook: A Guide to Techniques for Removing Bay Area Invasive Plants*, by Pete Holloran et al., 53–110. Berkeley, CA: The Watershed Project and California Invasive Plant Council, 2004.

Magness, Jodi. *The Archaeology of the Holy Land.* New York: Cambridge University Press, 2012.

———. "Ossuaries and the Burials of Jesus and James." *Journal of Biblical Literature* 124 (2005) 121–54.

———. "Were Sacrifices Offered at Qumran? The Animal Bone Deposits Reconsidered." *Journal of Ancient Judaism* 7 (2016) 5–34.

Manning, Samuel. *Those Holy Fields: Palestine.* London: Religious Tract Society, 1873.

Marshall, Taylor. "Was St. Simeon in Luke 2 Also the Son of Hillel the Rabbi?" *Dr. Taylor Marshall* (blog), Feb. 2017. https://taylormarshall.com/2017/02/st-simeon-luke-2-also-son-hillel-rabbi.html.

Martin, Ernest L. *Secrets of Golgotha: The Lost History of Jesus' Crucifixion.* Alhambra: Academy for Scriptural Knowledge, 1996.

———. *The Temples That Jerusalem Forgot.* Portland, OR: ASK, 2000.

Masterman, Ernest. "Emmaus." *International Standard Bible Encyclopedia Online*, 1939. https://www.internationalstandardbible.com/E/emmaus.html.

———. "Golgotha." *International Standard Bible Encyclopedia Online*, 1939. https://www.internationalstandardbible.com/G/golgotha.html.

———. "King's Dale." *International Standard Bible Encyclopedia Online*, 1939. https://www.internationalstandardbible.com/K/kings-vale.html.

Matt, Daniel C. *Becoming Elijah: Prophet of Transformation*. New Haven, CT: Yale University Press, 2022.

Maundress, Henry. *A Journey from Aleppo to Jerusalem (A.D. 1697)*. Oxford: The Theater, 1703.

McBirnie, William S. *The Search for the Authentic Tomb of Jesus*. 1975. Repr., Montrose, CA: Acclaimed, 1981.

McClintock, John, and James Strong. "Arimathea." *The Cyclopedia of Biblical, Theological, and Ecclesiastical Literature*, 1880. https://www.biblicalcyclopedia.com/A/arimatheea.html.

———. "Creed, Apostles." *The Cyclopedia of Biblical, Theological, and Ecclesiastical Literature*, 1880. https://www.biblicalcyclopedia.com/C/creed-apostles.html.

———. "Hebrews, the Epistle to The." *The Cyclopedia of Biblical, Theological, and Ecclesiastical Literature*, 1880. https://www.biblicalcyclopedia.com/H/hebrews-the-epistle-to-the.html.

———. "Hinnom." *The Cyclopedia of Biblical, Theological, and Ecclesiastical Literature*, 1880. https://www.biblicalcyclopedia.com/H/hinnom.html.

———. "Paulinus of Tyre." *The Cyclopedia of Biblical, Theological, and Ecclesiastical Literature*, 1880. https://www.biblicalcyclopedia.com/P/paulinus-of-tyre.html.

———. "Praetorium." *The Cyclopedia of Biblical, Theological, and Ecclesiastical Literature*, 1880. https://www.biblicalcyclopedia.com/P/praetorium.html.

———. "Ramathaimzophim." *The Cyclopedia of Biblical, Theological, and Ecclesiastical Literature*, 1880. https://www.biblicalcyclopedia.com/R/ramathaimzophim.html.

———. "Shaveh." *The Cyclopedia of Biblical, Theological, and Ecclesiastical Literature*, 1880. https://www.biblicalcyclopedia.com/S/shaveh.html.

McNamara, Martin. "Melchizedek: Gen. 14:17–20 in the Targums in Rabbinic and Early Christian Literature." *Biblica* 81 (2000) 1–31.

Mearns, P. "The Site of Emmaus." *Palestine Exploration Fund Quarterly Statement* 17 (Apr. 1885) 116–21.

Meyer, Marvin. *Judas: The Definitive Collection of Gospels and Legends About the Infamous Apostle of Jesus*. New York: HarperOne, 2007.

Milik, Jozef T. "Saint Thomas de Phordesa et Gen. 14:17." *Biblica* 42 (1961) 77–84.

Miller, Geoffrey. "Raphael the Liar: Angelic Deceit and Testing in the Book of Tobit." *Catholic Biblical Quarterly* 74 (July 2012) 492–508.

Milwaukee Public Museum. "Pottery Lamps: Open Saucer and Pinched Nozzle Lamps." Lamp Collections. Nov. 5, 2025. https://www.mpm.edu/index.php/research-collections/anthropology/anthropology-collections-research/mediterranean-oil-lamps/lamp-classifications.

Mishnah Shabbat. Sefaria. https://www.sefaria.org/Mishnah_Shabbat.6.10?lang=bi.

Mishnah Shekalim. Sefaria. https://www.sefaria.org/Mishnah_Shekalim.7.4?lang=bi.

Mosshammer, Alden A. "Easter and the Passover Moon: The Easter Computus and the Origins of the Christian Era." *Oxford Early Christian Studies* (Oct. 2008) 40–56.

Murphy-O'Connor, Jerome. "The First Letter to the Corinthians." In *The New Jerome Biblical Commentary*, edited by Raymond E. Brown et al., 798–815. Englewood Cliffs, NJ: Prentice Hall, 1996.

———. *The Holy Land: An Oxford Archaeological Guide from Earliest Times to 1700*. Kindle. New York: Oxford University Press, 2008.

Nagar, Yossi. "Skeletal Remains from the Excavations at Ketef Hinnom, Jerusalem." *Antiqot* 80 (2015) 55–58.

Nautin, Pierre. "L'Homelie de Meliton sur la Passion." *Revue d'Histoire Ecclésiastique* 44 (1949) 429–38.

Netzer, Ehud. *The Palaces of the Hasmoneans and Herod the Great*. Jerusalem: Yad Yihak Ben Zvi, 2001.

Newman, Hillel. "A Hippodrome on the Road to Ephrath." *Biblica* 86 (2005) 213–28.

Ngo, Robin. "Biblical Sha'arayim: Khirbet Qeiyafa's Second Gate Discovered." *Bible History Daily*, Jan. 5, 2017. https://www.biblicalarchaeology.org/daily/biblical-sites-places/biblical-archaeology-sites/biblical-shaarayim-khirbet-qeiyafa-second-gate/.

Ochser, Schulim, and Kaufmann Kohler. "Nicodemus." *The Jewish Encyclopedia*, 1906. https://jewishencyclopedia.com/articles/11525-nicodemus.

O'Connor, Colin. *Roman Bridges*. Cambridge: Cambridge University Press, 1993.

Opper, Thorsten. *Hadrian: Empire and Conflict*. Cambridge, MA: Harvard University Press, 2008.

Oren Cohen Group. "The Mount Zion Hotel." Nov. 5, 2025. https://www.orencohengroup.com/blog/mount-zion-hotel-early-20th-century-2/.

Papaioannou, Kim. *The Geography of Hell in the Teaching of Jesus: Gehenna, Hades, the Abyss, the Outer Darkness Where There Is Weeping and Gnashing of Teeth*. Eugene, OR: Pickwick, 2013.

Parsons, Mikeal. "Son and High Priest: A Study in the Christology of Hebrews." *Evangelical Quarterly* 60 (July/Sept. 1988) 195–216.

Paton, Lewis B. *Jerusalem in Bible Times*. Chicago: University of Chicago Press, 1908.

———. "The Third Wall of Jerusalem and Some Excavations on Its Supposed Line." *Journal of Biblical Literature* 24 (1905) 197–211.

Patrich, Joseph. "On the Lost Circus of Aelia Capitolina." *Scripta Classica Israelica* 21 (2002) 173–88.

Peleg-Barkat, Orit. "Herod's Western Palace in Jerusalem: Some New Insights." *Electrum* 26 (2019) 53–72.

Perdue, Robert E. "Arundo donax: Source of Musical Reeds and Industrial Cellulose." *Economic Botany* 12 (Oct./Dec. 1958) 368–404.

Perrot, J., et al. "Notes and News." *Israel Exploration Journal* 26 (1976) 47–58.

Phang, Sara. "The Families of Roman Soldiers (First and Second Centuries AD): Culture, Law, and Practice." *Journal of Family History* 27 (2003) 352–73.

Pierotti, Ermete. *Jerusalem Explored*. London: Bell and Daldy, 1864.

Pilgrim of Piacenza. *Of the Holy Places Visited by Antoninus Martyr*. Translated by Aubrey Stewart. London: Palestine Pilgrims' Text Society, 1887.

Pixner, Bargil. "Church of the Apostles Found on Mt. Zion." *Biblical Archaeology Review* 16 (May/June 1990) 17–35, 60. http://www.centuryone.org/apostles.html.

———. "The History of the 'Essene Gate' Area." *Zeitschrift Des Deutschen Palästina-Vereins* 105 (1989) 96–104.

———. "Jerusalem's Essene Gateway." *Biblical Archaeology Review* 23 (1997) 22–31, 64–66. http://www.centuryone.org/essene.html.

———. *Paths of the Messiah*. San Francisco: Ignatius, 2010.

Pollanen, M. S., and D. A. Chiasson. "Fracture of the Hyoid Bone in Strangulation: Comparison of Fractured and Unfractured Hyoids from Victims of Strangulation." *Journal of Forensic Science* 41 (Jan. 1996) 110–13.

Poloner, John. *John Poloner's Description of the Holy Land*. Translated by Aubrey Stewart. London: Palestine Pilgrims' Text Society, 1894.

Potter, David. *Constantine the Emperor*. New York: Oxford University Press, 2023.

Pringle, Denys. *The Churches of the Crusader Kingdom of Jerusalem: A Corpus*. Vol. 2, *L–Z (Excluding Tyre)*. New York: Cambridge University Press, 1998.

Pseudo-Tertullian. "Of the Harmony of the Old and New Laws." In *Ante-Nicene Fathers*, edited by Philip Schaff, 4:332–44. Repr., Grand Rapids: Christian Classics Ethereal Library, 2000.

Quintilian. *The Lesser Declamations*. Vol. 1. Translated by D. R. Shackleton Bailey. Cambridge, MA: Harvard University Press, 2006.

Rabinowitz, Gavin. "Archaeologists Find Battle Site Where Romans Breached Jerusalem Walls." *The Times of Israel*, Oct. 20, 2016. https://www.timesofisrael.com/archaeologists-find-battle-site-where-romans-breached-jerusalem-walls/.

Radley, Dario. "Ancient Garden Found at Jesus Christ's Burial Site, Verifying Biblical Account." *Archaeology News*, Apr. 6, 2025. https://archaeologymag.com/2025/04/ancient-garden-found-at-jesus-burial-site/.

Rahmani, Levi. *A Catalogue of Jewish Ossuaries in the Collections of the State of Israel*. Jerusalem: Israel Antiquities Authority and the Israel Academy of Sciences and Humanities, 1994.

Reed, Estelle. "Excavating at Mt. Zion: Jerusalem Dig Uncovers Ancient Mansion." *Bible History Daily*, July 18, 2015. https://www.biblicalarchaeology.org/daily/news/excavating-at-mt-zion-jerusalem-dig-uncovers-ancient-mansion/.

Reem, Amit. "First and Second Temple Period Fortifications and Herod's Palace in the Jerusalem Kishle Compound." In *Ancient Jerusalem Revealed: Archaeological Discoveries, 1998–2018*, edited by Hillel Geva, 136–44. Jerusalem: Israel Exploration Society, 2019.

———. "A Herodian-Period Staircase on Mt. Zion, Jerusalem, and a Reevaluation of the Remains from Bishop Gobat School." *Atiqot* 106 (2022) 89–128.

Reilly, Thomas. "Mount Calvary." *The Catholic Encyclopedia*, 1911. https://www.newadvent.org/cathen/03191a.htm.

Renan, Ernest. *The Life of Jesus*. Translated by Charles Edwin Wilbur. New York: Carleton, 1864.

Rhoads, David M. *Israel in Revolution 6–74 CE: A Political History Based on the Writings of Josephus*. Philadelphia: Fortress, 1976.

Riesner, Rainer. "Jesus, the Primitive Community, and the Essene Quarter of Jerusalem." In *Jesus and the Dead Sea Scrolls*, edited by J. H. Charlesworth, 198–234. New York: Doubleday, 1992.

Rijke, Alexandra. "Present Checkpoint Futures: the Relaunch of Checkpoint 300 in Bethlehem in the Occupied Palestinian Territories." *Geografiska Annaler Series B Human Geography* 103 (2021) 337–51.

Ro, Brandon. "Deciphering the 'Jesus Is Here' Cave—Early Christian Worship, Sacred Space, and Hierophany at Horvat Beit Loya." Tetrad Architecture and Planning, Apr. 8, 2025. https://brandonro.com/2025/04/08/deciphering-the-jesus-is-here-cave-early-christian-worship-sacred-space-and-hierophany-at-horvat-beit-loya/.

Roberts, Michael Symmons. "The Miracles of Jesus." BBC, Sept. 18, 2009. https://www.bbc.co.uk/religion/religions/christianity/history/miraclesofjesus_1.shtml.

Robinson, Edward, and Eli Smith. *Biblical Researches of Palestine and the Adjacent Regions: A Journal of Travels in the Year 1838*. Vol. 1. London: John Murray, 1841.

———. *Biblical Researches of Palestine and the Adjacent Regions: A Journal of Travels in the Years 1838 and 1852*. Vol. 2. London: John Murray, 1856.

Robinson, John C. "Crucifixion in the Roman World: The Use of Nails at the Time of Christ." *Studia Antiqua* 2 (2002) 25–59.

Rosovsky, Nitza. "In Jerusalem of the 1800s." *New York Times*, Oct. 18, 1987, sec. 10, 34.

Roth, Jonathan. *The Logistics of the Roman Army at War (264 B.C.—A.D. 235)*. Boston: Brill, 1999.

Rousseau, John, and Rami Arav. *Jesus and His World: An Archaeological and Cultural Dictionary*. Minneapolis: Fortress, 1995.

Saewulf. *Saewulf (1102, 1103 A.D.)*. Translated by C. Brownlow. London: Palestine Pilgrims' Text Society, 1892.

Safrai, Zeev. *The Beginnings of Christianity: A Collection of Articles*. Edited by Jack Pastor and Menachem Mor. Jerusalem: Yad Ben-Zvi, 2005.

Saller, Sylvester, and Bellarmino Bagatti. *The Town of Nebo (Khirbet el-Mekhayyat) with a Brief Survey of Other Ancient Christian Monuments in Transjordan*. Jerusalem: Franciscan, 1949.

Sandys, George. *Sandys Travels*. London: The Crown in Little Britain, 1673.

Schein, Bruce E. "The Second Wall of Jerusalem." *Biblical Archaeologist* 44 (1981) 21–26.

Schick, Conrad. "The Birthplace of John the Baptist." *Palestine Exploration Fund Quarterly Statement* 37 (Jan. 1905) 61–69.

———. "Boundary Between Judah and Benjamin." *Palestine Exploration Fund Quarterly Statement* 16 (July 1884) 181–87.

———. "Hill of 'Jeremiah's Grotto' Called by General Gordon 'Skull Hill.'" *Palestine Exploration Fund Quarterly Statement* 33 (Oct. 1901) 402–5.

———. "Mitteilungen aus Jerusalem." *Journal of the German Society for Exploration of Palestine* 1 (1878) 11–23.

Schiffer, Kathy. "Take a Journey Along Route 60: The Biblical Highway." *National Catholic Register*, Sept. 14, 2023. https://www.ncregister.com/blog/take-a-journey-along-route-60-the-biblical-highway.

Schmidt, Thomas C. *Josephus and Jesus: New Evidence for the One Called Christ*. New York: Oxford Academics, 2025.

Schofield, Alfred. *Where He Dwelt: Or Mind Pictures of Palestine*. Chicago: Rand McNally, 1914.

Schwarz, Yehoseph. *A Descriptive Geography and Brief Historical Sketch of Palestine*. Translated by Isaac Leeser. Philadelphia: A. Hart, 1850.

Second Anonymous Pilgrim. "Anonymous Pilgrim II (12th Century)." In *Anonymous Pilgrims, I–VIII (11th and 12th Centuries)*, translated by Aubrey Stewart, 5–12. London: Palestine Pilgrims' Text Society, 1894.

Shanks, Hershel. "Ancient Jerusalem: The Village, the Town, the City." *Bible History Daily*, Apr. 25, 2024. https://www.biblicalarchaeology.org/daily/biblical-sites/ancient-jerusalem/.

———. *Jerusalem: An Archaeological Biography*. New York: Random House, 1995.

———. "Scholar's Corner: New Analysis of the Crucified Man." *Bible History Daily*, Aug. 14, 2025. https://www.biblicalarchaeology.org/daily/biblical-topics/crucifixion/roman-crucifixion-methods-reveal-the-history-of-crucifixion/.

Shanks, Monte. *Papias and the New Testament*. Kindle. Eugene, OR: Pickwick, 2013.

Shimron, Aryeh, et al. "Petrochemistry of Sediment and Organic Materials Sampled from Ossuaries and Two Nails from the Tomb of the Family of the High Priest Caiaphas, Jerusalem." *Archaeological Discovery* 8 (2020) 260–87.

Shoemaker, Stephen. *Mary in Early Christian Faith and Devotion*. New Haven, CT: Yale University Press, 2016.

Silver, Sandra. *The Rise and Fall of the House of Herod*. Self-published, 2014.

Skarsaune, Oskar. *In the Shadow of the Temple: Jewish Influences on Early Christianity*. Downers Grove, IL: InterVarsity, 2002.

Skinner, Andrew. "A Historical Sketch of Galilee." *Brigham Young University Studies* 36 (1996) 113–25.

Smith, Ralph Allan. "Exegesis of the Great Commission." Theopolis Institute, Feb. 11, 2025. https://theopolisinstitute.com/exegesis-of-the-great-commission/.

Smyth, Kevin. "The Dead Sea Scrolls and Christianity: Ten Years After." *Studies: An Irish Quarterly Review* 50 (Spring 1961) 28–37.

Sobotta, Johannes. *Atlas and Textbook of Human Anatomy*. Vol. 3. Philadelphia: W. B. Saunders, 1906.

Soennecken, Katja. "Ramat Rahel in the Byzantine Period." MA thesis, University of Edinburgh, 2006.

Souvay, Charles. "Mount Olivet." *The Catholic Encyclopedia*, 1911. https://www.newadvent.org/cathen/11244b.htm.

Staples, Tim. "What Is Hell?" *Catholic Answers*, Nov. 8, 2011. https://www.catholic.com/magazine/online-edition/what-is-hell.

Steel, Ernest W., and Terence J. McGhee. *Water Supply and Sewerage*. Tokyo: McGraw-Hill, 1979.

Stegemann, H. *The Library of Qumran: On the Essenes, Qumran, John the Baptist, and Jesus*. Grand Rapids: Eerdmans, 1998.

Stein, Robert H. *The Method and Message of Jesus' Teachings*. Louisville: Westminster John Knox, 1995.

Steinmeyer, Nathan. "A Greek Hetaira in Hellenistic Jerusalem: 2,300-Year-Old Tomb of a Courtesan Uncovered in Jerusalem." *Bible History Daily*, Oct. 6, 2023. https://www.biblicalarchaeology.org/daily/ancient-israel/a-greek-hetaira-in-hellenistic-jerusalem/.

———. "Pontius Pilate and the Jerusalem Aqueduct." *Bible History Daily*, Dec. 24, 2021. https://www.biblicalarchaeology.org/daily/pontius-pilate-and-the-jerusalem-aqueduct/.

Stewart-Sykes, Alistair. *On Pascha*. New York: St. Vladimir's Seminary Press, 2001.

Sukenik, Eleazar L. "The Earliest Records of Christianity." *American Journal of Archaeology* 51 (1947) 351–65.

Sybrowsky, Rebecca L. "The Mount of Transfiguration." *Studia Antiqua* 2 (2003) 55–86.

Tabor, James. "Is This the Face of Jesus? Getting the Facts Straight on the Turin Shroud." YouTube video, July 11, 2025. https://www.youtube.com/watch?v=uXhkVCdr2KU.

———. *The Jesus Dynasty: The Hidden History of Jesus, His Royal Family, and the Birth of Christianity*. New York: Simon & Schuster, 2006.

———. "Locating Golgotha." *Religion Matters: From the Bible to the Modern World* (blog), Feb. 6, 2016. https://jamestabor.com/locating-golgotha/.

———. *The Lost Mary: Rediscovering the Mother of Jesus.* New York: Knopf, 2025.

———. "Part A Lecture: The Search for Jerusalem's Essene Gate and the Church of the Apostles." YouTube video, Mar. 23, 2022. https://www.youtube.com/watch?v=_P4Twtz1Pxw.

———. "Was Jesus a Carpenter?" *Religion Matters: From the Bible to the Modern World* (blog), Dec. 28, 2017. https://jamestabor.com/was-jesus-a-carpenter/.

Tabory, Joseph. "The Crucifixion of the Paschal Lamb." *Jewish Quarterly Review* 86 (Jan./Apr. 1996) 395–406.

Talmud Sanhedrin. Sefaria. https://www.sefaria.org/Sanhedrin.43a.21?lang=bi.

Talmud Shabbat. Sefaria. https://www.sefaria.org/Shabbat.104a.11?lang=bi.

Taylor, Jeremy. *The Whole Works of the Right Rev. Jeremy Taylor, D. D.* London: Henry G. Bohn, 1851.

Taylor, Joan. *Christians and the Holy Places: The Myth of Jewish Christian Origins.* New York: Clarendon, 1993.

———. *The Essenes, the Scrolls, and the Dead Sea.* Oxford: Oxford Academic, 2012.

———. "Golgotha: A Reconsideration of the Evidence for the Sites of Jesus' Crucifixion and Burial." *Bible and Spade* 15 (Spring 2002) 39–50. https://biblearchaeology.org/research/chronological-categories/life-and-ministry-of-jesus-and-apostles/2308-golgotha-a-reconsideration-of-the-evidence-for-the-sites-of-jesus-crucifixion-and-burial.

———, ed. *The Onomasticon by Eusebius of Caesarea.* Translated by G. Freeman-Grenville. Jerusalem: Carta, 2003.

Tenz, Johann M. "Calvary—Place of the Skull." *Palestine Exploration Fund Quarterly Statement* 43 (Oct. 1911) 189–92.

———. "Golgotha or Calvary—A Place of a Skull." *Palestine Exploration Fund Quarterly Statement* 30 (Oct. 1898) 248–49.

Theobald, Andrew. "The United Nations Truce Supervision Organization (UNTSO)." In *United Nations Peacekeeping Operations*, edited by Joachim A. Koops et al., 121–32. New York: Oxford University Press, 2015.

Theoderich. *Theoderich's Description of the Holy Places (Circa 1172 A.D.).* Translated by Aubrey Stewart. London: Palestine Pilgrims' Text Society, 1891.

Theodosius. *Theodosius (A.D. 530).* Translated by J. H. Bernard. London: Palestine Pilgrims' Text Society, 1893.

Thompson, Brent. "Archaeologist Recounts Discovery of Oldest Biblical Text." *Baptist Press*, Mar. 8, 2007. https://www.baptistpress.com/resource-library/news/archaeologist-recounts-discovery-of-oldest-biblical-text/.

Thurston, Herbert. "Apostles' Creed." *The Catholic Encyclopedia*, 1911. https://www.newadvent.org/cathen/01629a.htm.

———. "St. George." *The Catholic Encyclopedia*, 1911. https://www.newadvent.org/cathen/06453a.htm.

Toy, Crawford, and Kaufmann Kohler. "Joseph of Arimathea." *The Jewish Encyclopedia*, 1906. https://jewishencyclopedia.com/articles/8815-joseph-of-arimathaea.

Trites, Allison. "The Transfiguration of Jesus: The Gospel in Microcosm." *Evangelical Quarterly* 51 (1979) 67–79.

Turner, C. H. "The Early Episcopal Lists II." *Journal of Theological Studies* 1 (1900) 529–53.

Tzapheres, Vasileios. "The Monastery of the Cross." *Biblical Archaeology Review* 27 (2002) 32–41.

Uziel, Joe, and Shai Itzhaq. "Iron Age Jerusalem: Temple-Palace, Capital City." *Journal of the American Oriental Society* 127 (Apr./June 2007) 161–70.

Van de Velde, Charles. *Narrative of a Journey Through Syria and Palestine in 1851 and 1852*. Vol. 2. Edinburgh: William Blackwood and Sons, 1854.

Van Staalduine-Sulman, Eveline. *The Targum of Samuel: Studies in the Aramaic Interpretation of Scripture*. Leiden: Brill, 2002.

Vieweger, Dieter, et al. "DEI Excavations on the Southwestern Slope of Mount Zion (2015–2019)." *Archäologischer Anzeiger* 1 (2020) 1–76.

Vincent, John, et al. *The Man of Galilee*. New York: N. D. Thompson, 1894.

Voltaggio, Michele. "Xenodochia and Hospitia in Sixth-Century Jerusalem: Indicators for the Byzantine Pilgrimage to the Holy Places." *Zeitschrift Des Deutschen Palästina-Vereins* 127 (2011) 197–210.

Von Wahlde, Urban C. "The References to the Time and Place of the Crucifixion in 'Peri Pascha' of Melito of Sardis." *Journal of Theological Studies* 60 (Oct. 2009) 556–69.

Vuong, Lily C. *The Protoevangelium of James: Early Christian Apocrypha*. Eugene, OR: Cascade, 2019.

Wacks, Mel. *The Handbook of Biblical Numismatics*. Self-published, 2021.

Waheeb, Mohammed. "Mountain of Transfiguration and New Discoveries in Site of Jesus Baptism/Jordan River." *American International Journal of Contemporary Research* 9 (June 2019) 15–31.

Wallace-Hadrill, David S. *Eusebius of Caesarea*. London: A. R. Mowbray, 1960.

Warren, Charles. "Golgotha." In *A Dictionary of the Bible Dealing with Its Literature and Contents Including the Biblical Theology*, edited by James Hastings, 2:226. Edinburgh: T. & T. Clark, 1910.

Warren, Charles, and Claude Conder. *The Survey of Western Palestine: Jerusalem*. London: Committee of the Palestine Exploration Fund, 1884.

Watson, Charles M. "Commemoratorium de Casis dei Vel Monasteriis (Translation)." *Palestine Exploration Fund Quarterly Statement* 45 (Jan. 1913) 23–33.

———. "The Traditional Sites of Sion." *Palestine Exploration Fund Quarterly Statement* 42 (July 1910) 196–220.

Webster, Graham. *The Roman Imperial Army of the First and Second Centuries A.D.* Totowa, NJ: Barnes and Noble, 1985.

Weksler-Bdolah, Shlomit. *Aelia Capitolina—Jerusalem in the Roman Period: In Light of Archaeological Research.* Leiden: Brill, 2020.

Wenham, John W. "The Relatives of Jesus." *Evangelical Quarterly* 47 (Jan./Mar. 1975) 6–15.

Wilkinson, John. *Jerusalem Pilgrims Before the Crusades.* 3rd ed. Warminster, Eng.: Aris & Phillips, 2002.

Willibald. *The Hodoeporicon of Saint Willibald (Circa 754 A.D.).* Translated by Canon Brownlow. London: Palestine Pilgrims' Text Society, 1891.

Wilson, Charles W. *Golgotha and the Holy Sepulchre.* Edited by Charles M. Watson. London: Committee of the Palestine Exploration Fund, 1906.

———. *Ordnance Survey of Jerusalem.* Southampton: Her Majesty's Treasury, 1866.

Wilson, Charles W., and Stanley Lane-Poole. *Picturesque Palestine, Sinai, and Egypt.* New York: Appleton, 1884.

Wilson, Ian. *Murder at Golgotha: Revisiting the Most Famous Crime Scene in History.* Kindle. New York: St. Martin's, 2011.

Wilson, John. *The Lands of the Bible: Visited and Described in an Extensive Journey Undertaken with Special Reference to the Promotion of Biblical Research and the Advancement of the Cause of Philanthropy.* Vol. 1. Edinburgh: William Whyte, 1847.

Windle, Bryan. "Behold the Man: Where Did Pilate Sentence Jesus?" *Bible Archaeology Report*, Apr. 14, 2022. https://biblearchaeologyreport.com/2022/04/14/behold-the-man.

———. "Caiaphas: An Archaeological Biography." *Bible Archaeology Report*, Apr. 17, 2025. https://biblearchaeologyreport.com/2025/04/17/caiaphas-an-archaeological-biography/.

———. "Iron Age Judahite Administrative Complex Unearthed in Jerusalem." Associates for Biblical Research, July 24, 2020. https://biblearchaeology.org/current-events-list/4702-iron-age-judahite-complex.

———. "Traces of Ancient Garden Discovered Beneath the Church of the Holy Sepulcher." Associates for Biblical Research, Mar. 25, 2025. https://biblearchaeology.org/current-events-list/5218-traces-of-ancient-garden.

Woods, David. "On the Death of the Empress Fausta." *Greece and Rome* 45 (Apr. 1998) 70–86.

Woolliscroft, David J. *Roman Military Signaling.* Charleston, SC: Tempus, 2001.

Wright, N. T. *Luke for Everyone.* Louisville, KY: Westminster John Knox, 2004.

———. "Paul, Arabia, and Elijah (Galatians 1:17)." *Journal of Biblical Literature* 115 (Winter 1996) 683–92.

Yadin, Yigael. "A Note on Melchizedek and Qumran." *Israel Exploration Journal* 15 (1965) 152–54.

———. *The Scroll of the War of the Sons of Light Against the Sons of Darkness.* London: Oxford University Press, 1962.

———. *The Temple Scroll—The Hidden Law of the Dead Sea Sect.* New York: Random House, 1985.

Yechezkel, A., et al. "The Shaft Tunnel of the Biar Aqueduct of Jerusalem: Architecture, Hydrology, and Dating." *Geoarchaeology* (May 2021) 1–28. https://doi.org/10.1002/gea.21875.

Zhang, Deng, et al. "The Potential Application of Giant Reed (Arundo Donax) in Ecological Remediation." *Frontiers in Environmental Science* 9 (May 2021) Art. no. 652367.

Zionsberg Jerusalem. "The Gates." Mount Zion Excavations, Dec. 4, 2025. https://www.zionsberg-jerusalem.de/gate-of-the-essenes/.

Zissu, Boaz. "'Qumran Type' Graves in Jerusalem: Archaeological Evidence of an Essene Community?" *Dead Sea Discoveries* 5 (1998) 158–71.

www.ingramcontent.com/pod-product-compliance
Lightning Source LLC
LaVergne TN
LVHW050630100826
845148LV00011B/1820

* 9 7 9 8 3 8 5 2 7 1 3 8 2 *